GRADE 2

GRAPHIC ORGANIZERS
AND OTHER
VISUAL STRATEGIES

ENGAGE THE
BRAIN

D1473790

MARCIA L. TATE

CORWIN PRESS
Classroom

For information:

Corwin Press
A SAGE Publications Company
2455 Teller Road
Thousand Oaks, California 91320
CorwinPress.com

SAGE Publications, Ltd.
1 Oliver's Yard
55 City Road
London EC1Y 1SP
United Kingdom

SAGE Publications India Pvt. Ltd.
B 1/I 1 Mohan Cooperative
Industrial Area
Mathura Road, New Delhi
India 110 044

SAGE Publications Asia-Pacific Pvt. Ltd.
33 Pekin Street #02-01
Far East Square
Singapore 048763

Printed in the United States of America.

ISBN 978-1-4129-5226-2

This book is printed on acid-free paper.

08 09 10 11 12 10 9 8 7 6 5 4 3 2 1

Executive Editor: Kathleen Hex
Managing Developmental Editor: Christine Hood
Editorial Assistant: Anne O'Dell
Developmental Writer: Vicky Shiotsu
Developmental Editor: Kristine Johnson
Proofreader: Bette Darwin
Art Director: Anthony D. Paular
Cover Designer: Monique Hahn
Interior Production Artist: Karine Hovsepian
Illustrator: Jannie Ho
Design Consultant: PUMPKiN PIE Design

GRADE **2**

TABLE OF CONTENTS

Connections to Standards

This chart shows the national academic standards that are covered in each chapter.

MATHEMATICS	Standards are covered on pages
Numbers and Operations—Understand numbers, ways of representing numbers, relationships among numbers, and number systems.	11, 14, 16
Numbers and Operations—Understand meanings of operations and how they relate to one another.	9
Numbers and Operations—Compute fluently and make reasonable estimates.	16
Geometry—Analyze characteristics and properties of two- and three-dimensional geometric shapes, and develop mathematical arguments about geometric relationships.	18
Measurement—Understand measurable attributes of objects and the units, systems, and processes of measurement.	20
Data Analysis and Probability—Formulate questions that can be addressed with data, and collect, organize, and display relevant data to answer them.	23
Data Analysis and Probability—Select and use appropriate statistical methods to analyze data.	23
Data Analysis and Probability—Understand and apply basic concepts of probability.	25
Problem Solving—Build new mathematical knowledge through problem solving.	18
Problem Solving—Solve problems that arise in mathematics and in other contexts.	11
Connections—Recognize and use connections among mathematical ideas.	9, 14

SCIENCE	Standards are covered on pages
Science as Inquiry—Ability to conduct scientific inquiry.	34
Physical Science—Understand properties of objects and materials.	33, 34, 36
Life Science—Understand characteristics of organisms.	31
Life Science—Understand life cycles of organisms.	29
Life Science—Understand organisms and environments.	27
Earth and Space Science—Understand properties of earth materials.	38
Earth and Space Science—Understand changes in the earth and sky.	40
Science in Personal and Social Perspectives—Identify types of resources.	42

SOCIAL STUDIES	Standards are covered on pages
Understand culture and cultural diversity.	44, 61
Understand the ways human beings view themselves in and over time.	56
Understand the interactions among people, places, and environments.	53
Understand individual development and identity.	47, 56
Understand interactions among individuals, groups, and institutions.	47, 49, 51
Understand how people organize for the production, distribution, and consumption of goods and services.	58
Understand the ideals, principles, and practices of citizenship in a democratic republic.	61

LANGUAGE ARTS	Standards are covered on pages
Read a wide range of print and nonprint texts to build an understanding of texts, of self, and of the cultures of the United States and the world; to acquire new information; to respond to the needs and demands of society and the workplace; and for personal fulfillment (includes fiction and nonfiction, classic, and contemporary works).	67
Apply a wide range of strategies to comprehend, interpret, evaluate, and appreciate texts. Draw on prior experience, interactions with other readers and writers, knowledge of word meaning and of other texts, word identification strategies, and understanding of textual features (e.g., sound-letter correspondence, sentence structure, context, graphics).	63, 65, 76, 79
Adjust use of spoken, written, and visual language (e.g., conventions, style, vocabulary) to communicate effectively with a variety of audiences and for different purposes.	65, 67
Employ a wide range of strategies while writing, and use different writing process elements appropriately to communicate with different audiences for a variety of purposes.	69, 71
Apply knowledge of language structure, language conventions (e.g., spelling and punctuation), media techniques, figurative language, and genre to create, critique, and discuss print and nonprint texts.	69, 74, 77
Use a variety of technological and informational resources (e.g., libraries, databases, computer networks, video) to gather and synthesize information and to create and communicate knowledge.	79

Introduction

An ancient Chinese proverb claims: "Tell me, I forget. Show me, I remember. Involve me, I understand." This timeless saying insinuates what all educators should know: Unless students are involved and actively engaged in learning, true learning rarely occurs.

The latest brain research reveals that both the right and left hemispheres of the brain should be engaged in the learning process. This is important because the hemispheres talk to one another over the corpus callosum, the structure that connects them. No strategies are better designed for this purpose than graphic organizers and visuals. Both of these strategies engage students' visual modality. More information goes into the brain visually than through any other modality. Therefore, it makes sense to take advantage of students' visual strengths to reinforce and make sense of learning.

How to Use This Book

The activities in this book cover the content areas and are designed using strategies that actively engage the brain. They are presented in the way the brain learns best, to make sure students get the most out of each lesson: focus activity, modeling, guided practice, check for understanding, independent practice, and closing. Go through each step to ensure that students will be fully engaged in the concept being taught and understand its purpose and meaning.

Each step-by-step activity provides one or more visual tools students can use to make important connections between related concepts, structure their thinking, organize ideas logically, and reinforce learning. Graphic organizers and visuals include: place-value models, bar graph, network tree, concrete models, picture chart, idea web, Venn diagram, T-chart, newspapers, tally chart, collages, word cards, matrix, posters, circle chart, and more!

These brain-compatible activities are sure to engage and motivate every student's brain in your classroom! Watch your students change from passive to active learners as they process visual concepts into learning that is not only fun, but also remembered for a lifetime.

Put It Into Practice

Lecture and repetitive worksheets have long been the traditional way of delivering knowledge and reinforcing learning. While some higher-achieving students may engage in this type of learning, educators now know that actively engaging students' brains is not a luxury, but a necessity if students are truly to acquire and retain content, not only for tests, but for life.

The 1990s were dubbed the Decade of the Brain, because millions of dollars were spent on brain research. Educators today should know more about how students learn than ever before. Learning style theories that call for student engagement have been proposed for decades, as evidenced by research such as Howard Gardner's theory of multiple intelligences (1983), Bernice McCarthy's 4MAT Model (1990), and VAKT (visual, auditory, kinesthetic, tactile) learning styles theories.

I have identified 20 strategies that, according to brain research and learning style theory, appear to correlate with the way the brain learns best. I have observed hundreds of teachers—regular education, special education, and gifted. Regardless of the classification or grade level of the students, exemplary teachers consistently use these 20 strategies to deliver memorable classroom instruction and help their students understand and retain vast amounts of content.

These 20 brain-based instructional strategies include the following:

1. Brainstorming and Discussion

2. Drawing and Artwork

3. Field Trips

4. Games

5. Graphic Organizers, Semantic Maps, and Word Webs

6. Humor

7. Manipulatives, Experiments, Labs, and Models

8. Metaphors, Analogies, and Similes

9. Mnemonic Devices

10. Movement

11. Music, Rhythm, Rhyme, and Rap

12. Project-based and Problem-based Instruction

13. Reciprocal Teaching and Cooperative Learning

14. Role Plays, Drama, Pantomimes, Charades

15. Storytelling

16. Technology

17. Visualization and Guided Imagery

18. Visuals

19. Work Study and Apprenticeships

20. Writing and Journals

This book features Strategy 5: Graphic Organizers, Semantic Maps, and Word Webs, and Strategy 18: Visuals. Both of these strategies focus on integrating the visual and verbal elements of learning. Picture thinking, visual thinking, and visual/spatial learning is the phenomenon of thinking through visual processing. Since 90% of the brain's sensory input comes from visual sources, it stands to reason that the most powerful influence on learners' behavior is concrete, visual images. (Jensen, 1994) In addition, linking verbal and visual images increases students' ability to store and retrieve information. (Ogle, 2000)

Graphic organizers are visual representations of linear ideas that benefit both left and right hemispheres of the brain. They assist us in making sense of information, enable us to search for patterns, and provide an organized tool for making important conceptual connections. Graphic organizers, also known as word webs or semantic, mind, and concept maps, can be used to plan lessons or present information to students. Once familiar with the technique, students should be able to construct their own graphic organizers, reflecting their understanding of the concepts taught.

Because we live in a highly visual world, using visuals as a teaching strategy makes sense. Each day, students are overwhelmed with images from video games, computers, and television. Visual strategies capitalize specifically on the one modality that many students use consistently and have developed extensively—the visual modality. Types of visuals include overheads, maps, graphs, charts, and other concrete objects and artifacts that clarify learning. Since so much sensory input comes from visual sources, pictures, words, and learning-related artifacts around the classroom take on exaggerated importance in students' brains. Visuals such as these provide learning support and constant reinforcement.

These memorable strategies help students make sense of learning by focusing on the ways the brain learns best. Fully supported by the latest brain research, these strategies provide the tools you need to boost motivation, energy, and most important, the academic achievement of your students.

CHAPTER 1

Mathematics

Webs of Addition Facts: Fact Web

Skills Objectives

Use counters to generate addition facts.

Recognize addition facts for a particular sum.

Students need a firm grasp of basic number facts so they can perform higher-level computations. A **Fact Web** can help students gather and connect facts and commit them to memory.

1. Draw an oval on the board, and write *11* inside. Draw two more ovals and connect them to the center oval. Explain to students that webs can help them see how different facts relate to each other.

2. Give each student 20 counters. Have students place 11 counters in the middle of their desks and arrange them into two groups: five and six. Next, ask them to state two corresponding addition facts. *(5 + 6 = 11, 6 + 5 = 11)* Write *5 + 6* in one of the connecting ovals on the board and *6 + 5* in the other.

3. Have students continue to group 11 counters in different ways, and give addition facts. Write facts on the board in connected ovals.

4. Give students a copy of the **Webs of Addition Facts reproducible (page 10)**. Have them fill in facts, referring to the web on the board.

5. Have students fill in the webs by writing facts for sums 12 to 15, using counters to help them. You may want students to generate only those facts they need to memorize. Check that they are filling in their webs correctly.

6. Afterward, let students share their work. Compile the facts on butcher paper to make a class chart.

Extended Learning

Have students refer to their webs to write corresponding subtraction facts. For example, have them write subtraction facts that are related to the addition facts for 11 (e.g., *11 – 5 = 6, 11 – 8 = 3*).

> ### Materials
>
> Webs of Addition Facts reproducible
>
> counters (bingo chips, buttons, paper squares, or other small counters)
>
> butcher paper

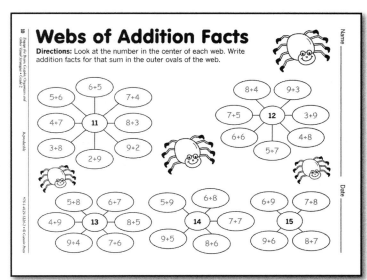

Webs of Addition Facts

Directions: Look at the number in the center of each web. Write addition facts for that sum in the outer ovals of the web.

Webs of Addition Facts

Directions: Look at the number in the center of each web. Write addition facts for that sum in the outer ovals of the web.

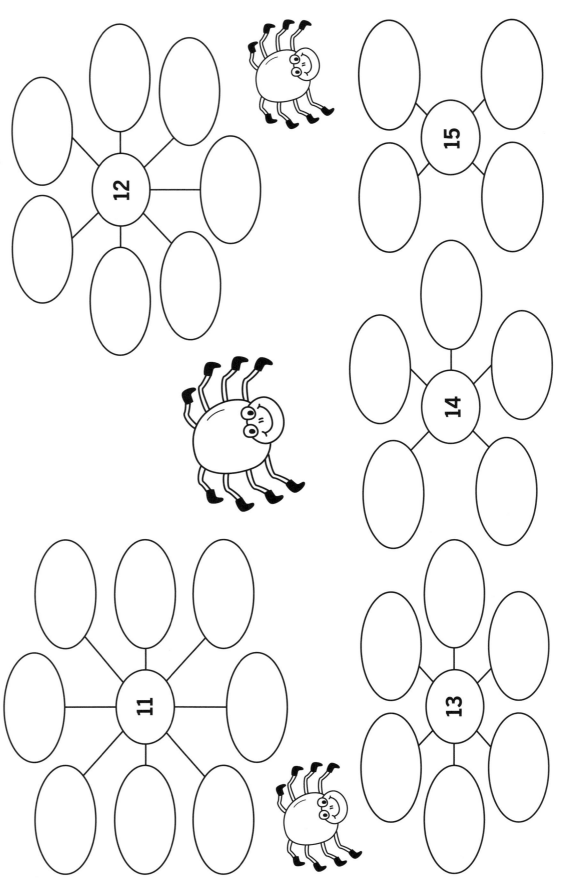

Engage the Brain: Graphic Organizers and Other Visual Strategies • Grade 2   978-1-4129-5226-2 • © Corwin Press

Jars of Beans: Counters

Skills Objectives
Estimate numbers of objects.
Make sets of tens to determine the number of objects.
Understand that the way we write numbers is based on groupings of ten.

Materials
Jars of Beans
reproducible

6 small jars with lids

dried beans
or jellybeans

masking tape

marker

paper cups

Counters and other manipulatives are an important part of the primary math curriculum. Manipulatives provide hands-on experiences that allow students to discover how numbers work. These concrete activities help develop the foundation students need to succeed in math. In this activity, students manipulate beans in a guessing game that reinforces estimation and place-value skills. Do the activity after you have introduced the concept of tens and ones.

1. Ahead of time, put various numbers (from 40 to 90) of beans in each of six small jars. Close the jars and use masking tape and a marker to label them *A–F*. Place Jars B–F in different areas of the classroom.

2. Tell students to raise their hands if they have ever saved a jar of pennies or coins. Ask them if it was difficult to count all the coins. Tell the class that you will show them an easy way to count large numbers of objects.

3. Hold up Jar A, and pass it around the room. Ask students to guess how many beans are inside. Write their guesses on the board.

4. Ask students to suggest how they can determine the number of beans without counting them one by one. Guide students to see that grouping the beans in sets of tens and ones can help them determine the number of beans.

5. Open the jar, and call on a student to count out ten beans into a paper cup. Ask a second student to count out ten more beans into a second cup. Continue the procedure until no more groups of ten can be made.

6. On the board, record the number of tens (the number of cups) and ones. Ask students: *How many beans were in the jar?* (For example, if there were 5 tens and 2 ones, students would know there were 52 beans.) Write the number on the board. To check that the number is correct, ask a student to count the beans one by one. The class will see that the two numbers match.

7. Distribute copies of the **Jars of Beans reproducible (page 13)**. Point out the columns on the chart, and work together to fill in the information for Jar A.

8. Direct students to move in small groups around the room and record how many beans they think are in the remaining jars. When everyone has made their estimates, have groups determine the actual amounts by opening the jars and grouping the beans into tens and ones. As students work, circulate around the room to check that they are completing their charts correctly.

9. Invite students to share their results with the class, and discuss the fact that the way numbers are written depends on how many sets of tens can be made.

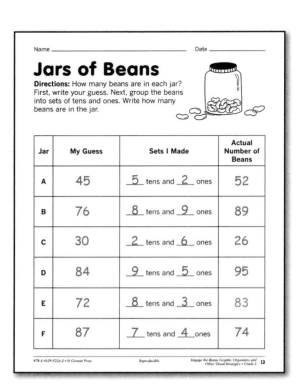

Name _____ Date _____

Jars of Beans

Directions: How many beans are in each jar? First, write your guess. Next, group the beans into sets of tens and ones. Write how many beans are in the jar.

Jar	My Guess	Sets I Made	Actual Number of Beans
A	45	_5_ tens and _2_ ones	52
B	76	_8_ tens and _9_ ones	89
C	30	_2_ tens and _6_ ones	26
D	84	_9_ tens and _5_ ones	95
E	72	_8_ tens and _3_ ones	83
F	87	_7_ tens and _4_ ones	74

978-1-4129-5226-2 • © Corwin Press   Reproducible   Engage the Brain: Graphic Organizers and Other Visual Strategies • Grade 2   **13**

Name _____ Date _____

Jars of Beans

Directions: How many beans are in each jar? First, write your guess. Next, group the beans into sets of tens and ones. Write how many beans are in the jar.

Jar	My Guess	Sets I Made	Actual Number of Beans
A		_____ tens and _____ ones	
B		_____ tens and _____ ones	
C		_____ tens and _____ ones	
D		_____ tens and _____ ones	
E		_____ tens and _____ ones	
F		_____ tens and _____ones	

Place Value: Place-Value Models

Materials

dried pinto beans

craft sticks

craft glue

Skills Objectives

Understand that numbers are written based on place-value groupings.
Identify a three-digit number based on the number of hundreds, tens, and ones.
Understand the function of zero as a place holder.

Concrete **Place-Value Models** are essential for helping students understand the number system. If commercial models are not available, allow students to make their own using craft sticks and dried pinto beans. This activity gives directions for making the models as well as suggestions for using them.

Making Ten-Sticks

1. Ask students if they can think of a way to show 24 beans. Tell them they will make models that will help show large numbers. Divide the class into small groups, and provide each group with craft sticks, pinto beans, and bottles of glue. Instruct each student in the group to take ten craft sticks.

2. Tell students to glue ten beans on each stick. Demonstrate how to do this by carefully dabbing some glue onto the stick and gluing the beans in a row.

3. Let the sticks dry thoroughly before using. (See "Making Hundred-Squares" on page 15.)

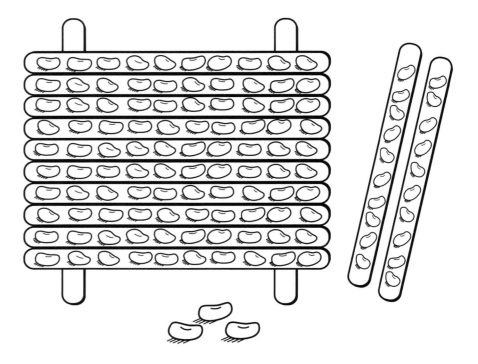

Making Hundred-Squares

1. Divide the class into groups of at least five students. Have students bring their ten-sticks to their group.

2. Show students how to make hundred-squares with some of their ten-sticks. For one square, place two craft sticks about three inches apart. Then place ten ten-sticks side by side across the two sticks to form a "raft," or hundred-square. Glue the sticks in place. Direct each group to make four hundred-squares.

Working with Place-Value Models

Place-value models help students conceptualize numbers. Concrete activities such as counting, grouping, and recording help students see the connection between written numbers and the amounts they represent. Let students work in groups and use their place-value models (hundred-squares, ten-sticks, and single beans) as you lead them through the following activities:

1. Tell students to lay out 2 hundreds, 3 tens, and 5 ones. Ask how many beans there are all together, and have students write the number (235) on a sheet of paper. Instruct students to hold up their papers so you can check the numbers they wrote. Continue the procedure with other place-value groupings.

2. Write *374* on the board. Ask students to arrange their models to match the number. Repeat the activity several times with different numbers.

3. Write *320* the board. Ask students to arrange their models to match the number. Point out that the *0* is needed as a placeholder to show that the *3* refers to 3 hundreds and the *2* refers to 2 tens. Without the *0*, the number would be confused with 32, a completely different amount. Continue the activity by having students use their models to display the following amounts: 320, 302, 230, and 203.

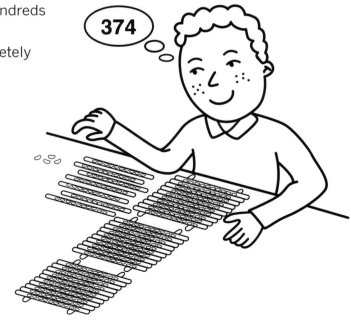

4. Check that students understand the concept of 0 in place value by having them arrange their models to show the difference between 40 and 400, 105 and 150, and other similar numbers. Have groups take turns holding up their models to show the value of each number as you check for understanding.

Money Matters: Concept Wheel

Materials

Money Wheel reproducible

containers of play coins

Skills Objectives

Recognize the value of individual coins.
Combine coins to make determined amounts.
Recognize equivalent amounts.

A **Concept Wheel** displays facts or attributes associated with a single topic or concept. Like a web, it can be used to display various aspects of a topic. In this activity, the concept wheel reinforces the idea that different coin combinations can have the same value. Do the activity after students have learned the value of coin combinations.

1. Hold up a quarter. Ask students to name the value of the coin. Ask what other coins make that same amount. Tell students they will find different ways to make the same amounts.

2. Pair up students, and give each pair a container of play coins. Write *45¢* on the board. Tell students to display the amount with their coins.

3. Ask volunteers to name the coins they used and then draw them (circles with designated amounts) on the board. Elicit as many responses as possible. Discuss that there are many different ways to get the same amount.

4. Draw a wheel on the board like that shown on the **Money Wheel reproducible (page 17)**. Write *62¢* in the center of the wheel. Next, have students use their coins to make two different combinations equaling 62¢. Then have them state their combinations as you draw their responses in the outer sections of the wheel.

5. Give students a copy of the Money Wheel reproducible. Assign each pair an amount. Have pairs write their amount in the center of the wheel and draw matching coin combinations around it.

6. Display completed wheels so students can compare their work.

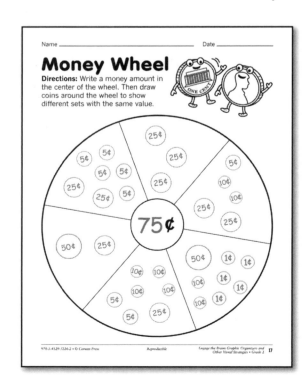

Name _____ Date _____

Money Wheel

Directions: Write a money amount in the center of the wheel. Then draw coins around the wheel to show different sets with the same value.

75¢

978-1-4129-5226-2 • © Corwin Press   Reproducible   *Engage the Brain: Graphic Organizers and Other Visual Strategies • Grade 2* **17**

Money Wheel

Directions: Write a money amount in the center of the wheel. Then draw coins around the wheel to show different sets with the same value.

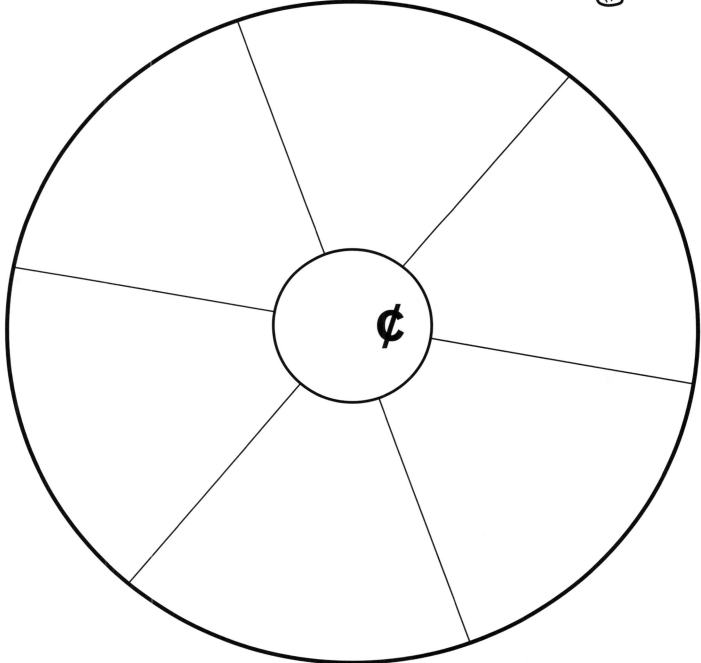

Properties of Geometric Solids: Matrix

Materials

Slide, Roll, Stack reproducible

assortment of geometric solids (toy blocks, soup cans, and other common objects)

chart paper

Skills Objectives

Observe and compare properties of geometric solids.
Identify common features of solids.

A **Matrix** can display the attributes of many items. Because the data is organized into columns and rows, students can quickly glean information and make comparisons. In this activity, students use a matrix to compare geometric solids.

1. Make an enlarged version of the **Slide, Roll, Stack reproducible (page 19)** on chart paper. Display the chart. Hold up each of the solids, and ask the class to name it.

2. Review some of the properties students have already learned about solids. Tell them they will discover some other properties.

3. Give students a copy of the Slide, Roll, Stack reproducible. Then divide the class into small groups, and provide each group with a few geometric solids.

4. Tell students to find a cube. Instruct them to push the cube to see if it will slide or roll. (It slides.) Have students see if they can stack two cubes. (They stack.) Discuss results.

5. Ask volunteers to write *yes* or *no* in the first row of the chart to show what they learned about the cube. Then have students move on to the rectangular prism. Ask them to predict if the figure will slide, roll, or stack.

6. Have students fill in the chart as they experiment with the rectangular prism and remaining figures. Make sure they understand how to complete the chart.

7. Have students share their results, and write them on the class chart. Discuss which figures could slide, roll, and stack. Ask students to determine which features allow solids to slide, roll, or stack. (Figures with flat surfaces can slide; those with curved surfaces can roll; those that sit upright can stack.)

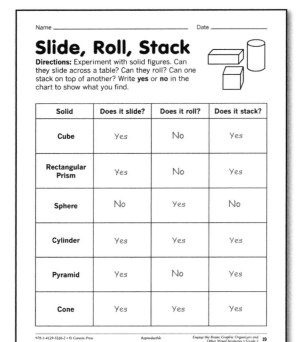

Name _____ Date _____

Slide, Roll, Stack

Directions: Experiment with solid figures. Can they slide across a table? Can they roll? Can one stack on top of another? Write **yes** or **no** in the chart to show what you find.

Solid	Does it slide?	Does it roll?	Does it stack?
Cube	Yes	No	Yes
Rectangular Prism	Yes	No	Yes
Sphere	No	Yes	No
Cylinder	Yes	Yes	Yes
Pyramid	Yes	No	Yes
Cone	Yes	Yes	Yes

Name _____ Date _____

Slide, Roll, Stack

Directions: Experiment with solid figures. Can they slide across a table? Can they roll? Can one stack on top of another? Write **yes** or **no** in the chart to show what you find.

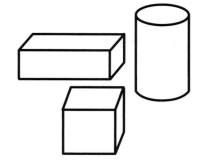

Solid	Does it slide?	Does it roll?	Does it stack?
Cube			
Rectangular Prism			
Sphere			
Cylinder			
Pyramid			
Cone			

Sky-High Words: Network Tree

Materials

Sky-High Words reproducible

measuring tools and containers (measuring tapes, rulers, balance scales, measuring cups, calendars, thermometers, clocks, milk jugs)

colored pencils (optional)

Skills Objectives

Demonstrate understanding of various units of measure.
Recognize that different kinds of measurements require different units of measure.

A **Network Tree** is helpful for organizing information when a single topic needs to be split into several subtopics, with each subtopic branching into further categories. A network tree helps students see how several different topics or ideas are interrelated. In this activity, students use a network tree to organize measurement terms. Do the activity after students have experienced measuring various items.

1. Write the following questions on the board: *How long is the desk? How heavy is it?* Tell students that these questions can be answered using measurement. Then guide the class into helping you add more questions on the board. For example: *How much water will it hold? How hot is it today? How far is school from your home? What time is it?*

2. Point to the questions, and explain that each kind of measurement is described with certain units of measure. Remind students that each unit of measure describes only one kind of measurement: inches describe length, pounds describe weight, liters describe capacity, and so on.

3. Set out measuring tools and containers around the room. (Students should be familiar with them because of their prior measuring experiences.) Direct students to examine the objects and list the units of measure they see (e.g., inch, foot, centimeter, cup, liter, and so on).

4. After students have examined the objects, brainstorm the different kinds of measurements people make (e.g., length and weight) as well as the corresponding units of measure (e.g., foot and meter for length). Write students' ideas on the board. Following are some suggestions:

   • Length (Width, Height)—inch, foot, yard, mile, centimeter, meter
   • Weight—ounce, pound, gram, kilogram
   • Capacity—cup, pint, quart, gallon, liter
   • Time—second, minute, hour, month, day, year
   • Temperature—degrees Fahrenheit, degrees Celsius

5. Give students a copy of the **Sky-High Words reproducible (page 22)**. Tell students that they are going to make a "tree" that connects units of measure that belong together.

6. Point out the three boxes at the top of the page. Instruct students to write three measurements of their choice, such as *Length*, *Weight*, and *Capacity*. Have students fill in the remaining boxes with the corresponding units of measure. (If you want students to distinguish metric units from standard units, they can underline one of the units with different colored pencils.)

7. Display students' work in the classroom, along with the appropriate measuring tools.

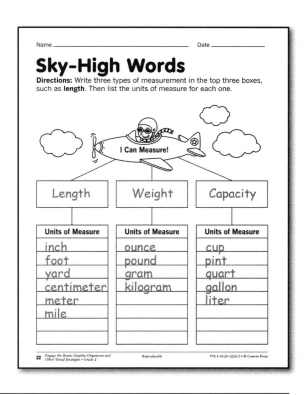

Name _____   Date _____

Sky-High Words

Directions: Write three types of measurement in the top three boxes, such as **length**. Then list the units of measure for each one.

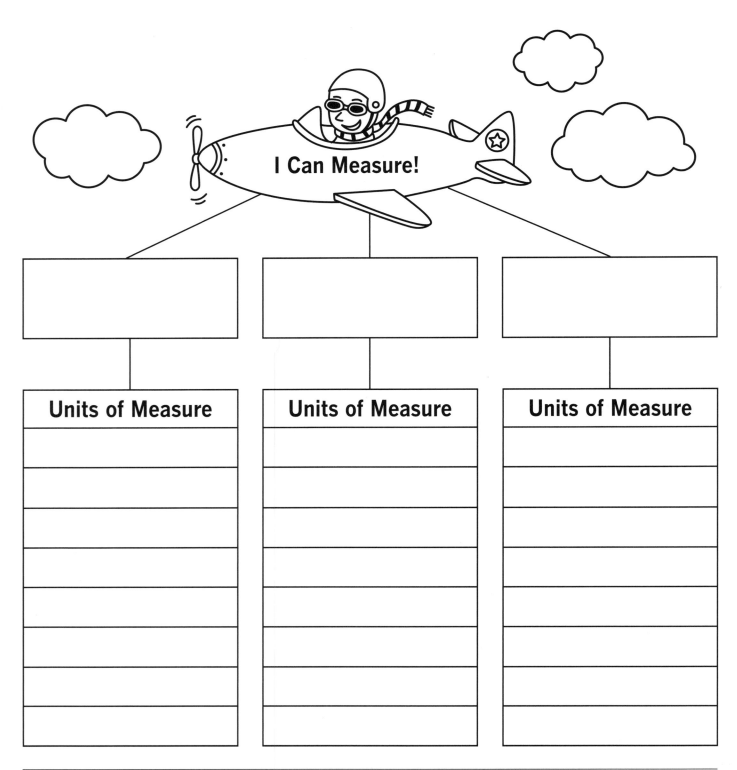

I Can Measure!

Units of Measure	Units of Measure	Units of Measure

 Engage the Brain: Graphic Organizers and Other Visual Strategies • Grade 2   *Reproducible*   978-1-4129-5226-2 • © Corwin Press

Comparing Families: Bar Graph

Skills Objectives
Collect and organize data on a bar graph.
Read information on a bar graph.
Analyze and draw conclusions from a set of data.

Materials

2" colored paper squares

2" x 12" strips of white construction paper

butcher paper

markers

glue

tape

Graphs present facts in a visual form that makes reading and comparing data easier. **Bar Graphs** are especially useful for primary students because of their concrete nature; students simply compare bar lengths to establish which ones represent greater or smaller quantities. This activity uses family sizes as the basis for creating a graph. Once the graph is completed, students can read the data to draw conclusions about their families. Organizing, reading, and analyzing data are important activities for developing students' understanding of statistics and how they are used.

1. Ask six students to tell how many people are in their families. Write their responses on the board, and direct the class to look at the numbers and note that family sizes vary. Then ask students if there is another way to show different family sizes. Guide them to realize that a graph can help them compare family sizes quickly and easily. Using the names of your family members, draw on the board a bar similar to one of those shown below.

2. Give each student a strip of white construction paper. Then have students take a colored paper square for each member of their family. Instruct them to use markers to write the names of family members on the squares.

3. Tell students to glue the squares onto their white strips, beginning with the square with their name. Show them how to glue the squares so they touch to form a line. (To make a vertical bar graph, have students stack squares on top of each other to make a vertical bar. For a horizontal bar graph, have students glue squares side by side to form a horizontal bar.) When all the squares are in place, instruct students to trim the excess white paper.

Janet	Kelly	Mom	Dad

Dad
Mom
Kelly
Janet

4. Direct students to tape their strips along the edge of a sheet of butcher paper to form a class bar graph. Have the class tape the strips in order according to size, beginning with the shortest strips and ending with the longest.

5. Display the butcher paper on a bulletin board or the wall. Point out that the bars increase in size. Discuss what the bars represent (family sizes). Then have the class look at the graph to answer questions such as the following:

- *Who has the largest family? How many members are in that family?*
- *Who has the smallest family? How many members are in that family?*
- *How many students have five people in their family?*
- *How many students have fewer than four people in their family?*
- *Which students have six people in their family?*
- *Which is greater—the number of students with three family members or the number of students with six family members?*
- *How many family members do most students have?*
- *Do more families have girl children or boy children?*

				Dad
		Grandpa	Mom	Mom
Nana	Dad	Grandma	Dad	Jerome
Mom	Mom	Mateo	Brit	Cherie
Kara	Dylan	Lea	Lisa	Ryan

Heads or Tails: Tally Chart

Skills Objectives
Predict what will happen in a probability experiment.
Conduct a probability experiment.
Make a tally chart to record the results of a probability experiment.

Materials
Heads or Tails reproducible

pennies

work mats (placemats, felt squares, construction paper)

A **Tally Chart** lets students keep track of data easily. Often used as a score-keeping tool in games, tallies are also used for record-keeping purposes in probability experiments. In this activity, students will make a tally chart to record the results of a penny toss.

1. Hold up a penny for the class, and have students identify the two sides as heads and tails. Tell the class that when a penny is tossed, it can land either heads up or tails up.

2. Write *heads* and *tails* on the board. Then demonstrate by tossing the penny. Call on a student to identify how the penny lands. On the board, make a tally mark under *heads* if the penny lands heads up, and under *tails* if it lands tails up. Repeat the procedure three more times, and discuss the results.

3. Give each student a mat, a penny, and a copy of the **Heads or Tails reproducible (page 26)**. Read Step 1 together, and have students check one box to predict what they think will happen if they toss a penny 20 times. Ask students how they made their predictions.

4. Have students follow Steps 2 and 3 on their reproducible to do their penny toss experiment. Remind them that they will make a tally mark each time, so they should have 20 tallies by the end of the activity. The tallies will help them keep track of their results.

5. Afterward, let students share their tally charts and compare the results. Ask the class to determine if one kind of result seemed to occur more frequently than the others. Explain that scientists often do experiments many times to find out what results are most likely to happen.

Heads or Tails

tails   heads

Step 1

Think about how a penny will land when you toss it 20 times. Which do you think will happen? Check one of the boxes to show your answer.

☐ It will always land heads up.

☐ It will always land tails up.

☐ It will land heads up most of the time.

☐ It will land tails up most of the time.

☐ It will land heads up and tails up the same number of times.

Step 2

Now get a penny and a mat. Toss the penny 20 times on the mat. Make a tally mark on the chart each time to show how the penny landed.

How the Penny Landed	Tally
heads up	
tails up	

Step 3

Look at your tally chart and answer the questions.

How many times did the penny land heads up? _____

How many times did the penny land tails up? _____

CHAPTER 2

Science

Living Things in My Neighborhood: Network Tree

Skills Objectives

Identify plants and animals in the immediate environment.
Recognize that living things thrive in different environments.

Materials
My Chart of Living
Things reproducible

Most students have an intuitive idea about living versus nonliving things. Categorizing living things helps students understand and appreciate the many species that inhabit their world. In this activity, students identify living things around them and display the information on a **Network Tree** as a hierarchy of concepts.

1. Have students look out the window and describe what they see. Write their responses on the board (e.g., *people, trees, grass, cats, birds*). Point out that many living things share an environment with people and can be grouped into two main categories—plants and animals. Have students classify their responses as plants or animals. Group their ideas on the board in a network tree.

2. Give students a copy of the **My Chart of Living Things reproducible (page 28)**. For homework, instruct them to look around their neighborhood for living things and draw three plants and three animals on their chart. Have them label the pictures using specific names, such as *pine tree* or *ladybug*. Generic names such as *tree* or *insect* are also fine if specifics are unknown.

3. Have students bring their charts to school to share with the class.

Extended Learning

Compile the information from students' charts to make two larger charts. Write *Plants* on one sheet of chart paper and *Animals* on another. Have students call out plants and animals from their charts, while you list them on your charts. Help students see that their environment supports a variety of living things.

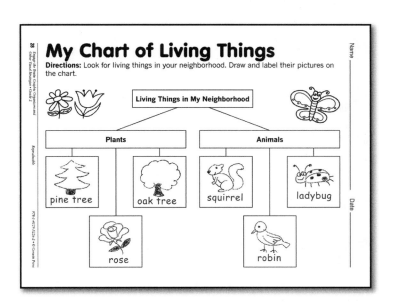

Name _____ Date _____

My Chart of Living Things

Directions: Look for living things in your neighborhood. Draw and label their pictures on the chart.

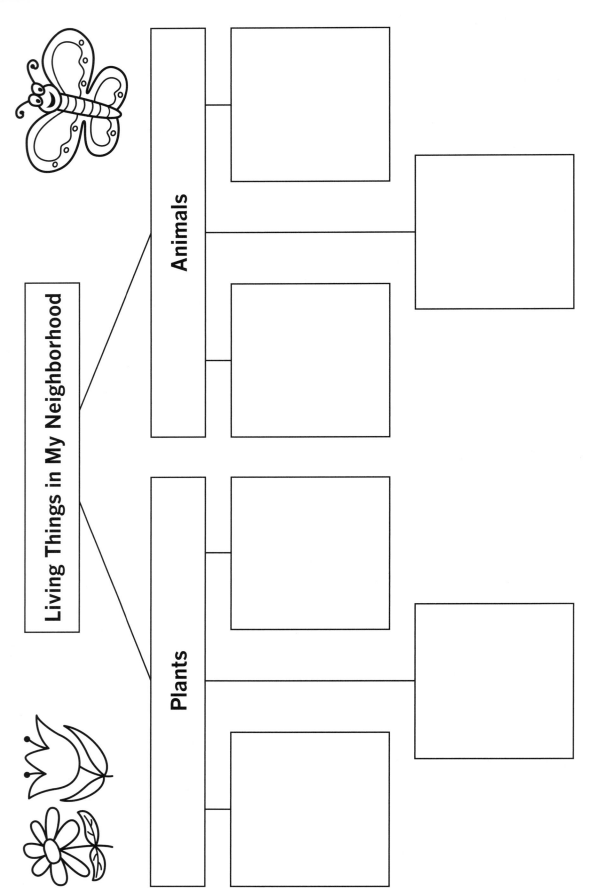

Living Things in My Neighborhood

Animals

Plants

Engage the Brain: Graphic Organizers and Other Visual Strategies • Grade 2   *Reproducible*   978-1-4129-5226-2 • © *Corwin Press*

The Cycles of Life: Cycle Chart

Skills Objectives

Demonstrate knowledge of stages of growth.

Read for information.

Record events in sequential order.

Materials

Life Cycle Chart reproducible

pictures of various baby and adult animals

books, magazines, and other resources that show how animals develop (*See How They Grow* series, published by Dorling Kindersley, is an excellent resource)

A **Cycle Chart** shows how a series of events occur repeatedly as well as sequentially. This graphic organizer is ideal for illustrating how one event leads to another. In this activity, each student researches the life cycle of an animal and presents four stages of growth.

1. Show pictures of animals as babies and adults. Help students see that some baby animals (e.g., elephant, giraffe) resemble their parents, while others (e.g., butterfly, frog) do not. Tell students that all baby animals grow and change, regardless of how they look at birth.

2. Discuss how animals go through different stages of growth. These stages make up an animal's life cycle. Then draw a copy of the **Life Cycle Chart reproducible (page 30)** on the board. Discuss the four stages in a person's life (baby, child, teenager, adult), and draw these stages on the board. Add a brief sentence describing each stage: *A baby is born. The baby becomes a child. The child grows into a teenager. The teenager becomes an adult.*

3. Tell students that they will be drawing the four stages of an animal's life. Then distribute copies of the Life Cycle Chart reproducible. Provide books, magazines, and other resources for researching different animals' life stages. Direct each student to choose an animal and complete the graphic organizer.

4. Circulate around the room as students work on their Life Cycle Charts. Ask questions to evaluate student learning, such as: *How did you decide which stages to show? What did you find out that you didn't know before?*

5. When students are finished, invite them to present their charts to the class.

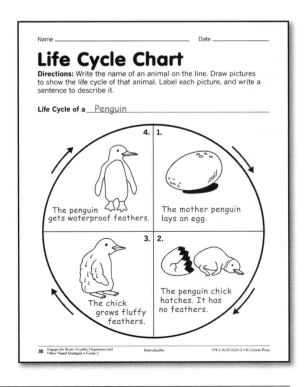

Name _____ Date _____

Life Cycle Chart

Directions: Write the name of an animal on the line. Draw pictures to show the life cycle of that animal. Label each picture, and write a sentence to describe it.

Life Cycle of a Penguin

4. The penguin gets waterproof feathers.

1. The mother penguin lays an egg.

3. The chick grows fluffy feathers.

2. The penguin chick hatches. It has no feathers.

30 *Engage the Brain: Graphic Organizers and Other Visual Strategies • Grade 2*   Reproducible   978-1-4129-5226-2 • © Corwin Press

Name _____ Date _____

Life Cycle Chart

Directions: Write the name of an animal on the line. Draw pictures to show the life cycle of that animal. Label each picture, and write a sentence to describe it.

Life Cycle of a _____

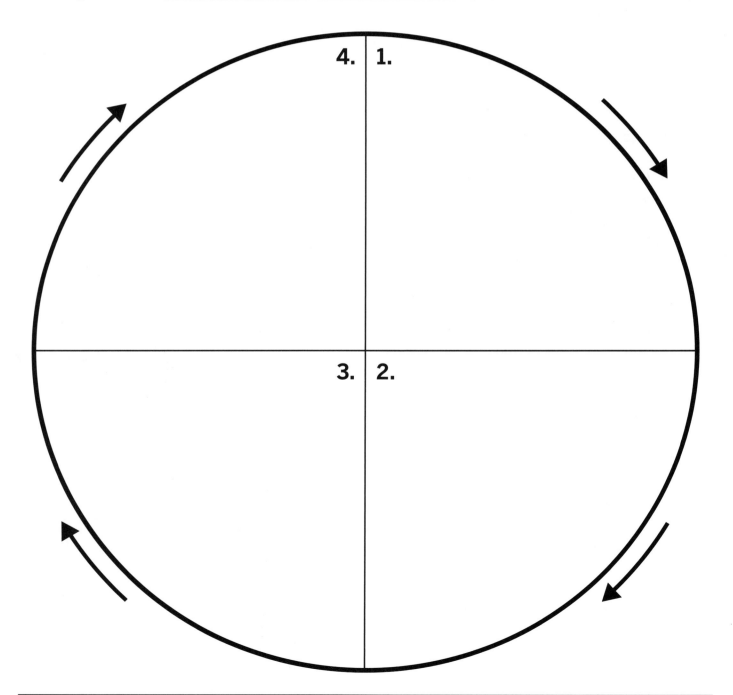

We're Growing! Concrete Models

Skills Objectives
Recognize one's own physical growth.
Measure and compare length.

Materials

tape measures

masking tape

yarn

butcher paper

scissors

Young students are keenly interested in their growth. They are excited to find out how tall they are or to see how far they can reach up with their hands. Therefore, concrete expressions of growth—such as growth charts parents mark yearly to track their children's heights—are fun and intriguing to children. But these **Concrete Models** serve another purpose; they are an effective tool for helping students see how much their bodies grow and change over time.

1. Ask students to describe how their bodies have changed since they were babies. Elicit from the class the idea that all of them have grown a great deal since birth. Tell students that people—like all living things—grow and change as they become adults.

2. For homework, have students find out how many inches long they were at birth. Direct each student to record the information on a sheet of paper and bring it to school.

3. Tape several tape measures to a wall so the ends line up with the floor. Then pair up students and have partners take turns measuring each other's heights. (Instruct students to take off their shoes before being measured.) Have them record their height on the paper they brought from home.

4. Give each student a length of yarn. Ask students to cut two lengths—one that shows their length at birth and one that shows their current height. Check that students understand how to proceed by having them show you "thumbs up" or "thumbs down."

5. Have students tape their lengths of yarn to a sheet of butcher paper. Instruct them to tape their pieces of yarn side by side and label the lengths. (The bottom end of each length of yarn should touch the edge of the butcher paper.) Have students write their names to identify their yarn lengths.

6. Ask students to look at the display and answer the following questions to initiate a discussion on childhood growth patterns: *How many inches have you grown since birth? Who grew the most since birth? Based on the graph, do you think those who are longer at birth grow into taller adults?*

Extended Learning

- Have students bring in three photos of themselves at different ages. One of their photos should be current. Then have students tape their photos to colored paper and label their pictures with their names and ages. Display the photos on a bulletin board titled *We're Growing!*

- Ask students to list things they can do now that they couldn't do as a preschooler (e.g., *I can read; I can ride a bike*). Explain that children grow in many ways: they grow physically; they learn new skills; and they understand more difficult concepts. Then have students make another list showing the things they can't do now but hope to do when they become older. Let students compare their lists with one another.

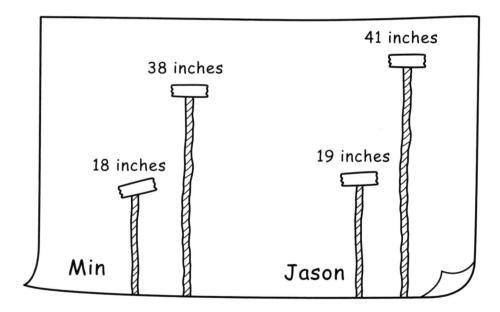

Three Forms of Matter: Concrete Objects

Skills Objectives
Identify the three forms of matter and their properties.
Classify objects as solid, liquid, or gas.

Science involves exploration of the physical world. When introducing science lessons, use **Concrete Objects** as often as possible to help students make the connection between the scientific concept and the physical environment in which they live. This activity utilizes concrete objects to illustrate the three forms of matter.

1. Have students name several items in the classroom. Tell them that everything in the room is made up of *matter*. Explain that there are three forms of matter.

2. Hold up a ruler and a sheet of paper, and explain that the two objects are *solids*. Then display a glass of water and a container of juice. Explain that water and juice are *liquids*. Finally, show an inflated balloon and a beach ball. Explain that the objects are "puffed up" because air is inside. Air is an invisible *gas*.

3. Brainstorm the characteristics of solids, liquids, and gases. Guide the class to see that solids have shape while liquids and gases do not. Liquids take on the shape of their containers; gases spread out to fill the space inside their containers.

4. Divide the class into small groups, and have each group cut out magazine pictures showing the three forms of matter. (Since gases might be difficult to find, have students look for pictures of objects that are filled with air, such as balloons, tires, and bubbles.)

5. Have each group glue their pictures to construction paper to make a poster titled *Solids, Liquids, Gases*. Display the posters around the classroom.

Materials
solids (ruler, sheet of paper)

liquids (glass of water, clear container of juice)

gases (inflated balloon, beach ball)

scissors

old magazines

construction paper

How Much Light? Three-Column Chart

Materials

How Much Light? reproducible

sheet of black construction paper, waxed paper, and plastic wrap

testing materials (felt squares, fabric swatches, tissue paper, food containers, food storage bags, wrapping paper)

3 trays or tubs

Skill Objective

Recognize that different types of materials allow different amounts of light to pass through.

Using a chart divided into columns is an effective way to organize data that involves the traits of many items. In this activity, students observe how much light passes through various kinds of materials and record their observations in a **Three-Column Chart**.

1. Ask a student to hold up a sheet of black construction paper. Put your hand behind the paper. Ask students: *Can you see my hand?* They can't. Explain that the black paper blocks light from passing through.

2. Ask another student to hold up a sheet of plastic wrap, and hold up your hand behind it. Tell students that this time your hand is visible because the plastic wrap lets all of the light through.

3. Repeat Step 1 using a sheet of waxed paper. Students will see your hand, but it will look "frosty." Explain that the waxed paper lets only some light through.

4. Give students a copy of the **How Much Light? reproducible (page 35)**, and explain that they will be testing different materials. Divide the class into small groups, and provide each group with various materials to test. Direct the class to do the "hand test" to determine how much light passes through each material. Students may also test the materials by holding them up to the light, but remind them never to look directly at the light source.

5. When all the materials have been tested, have the class sort them into three trays or tubs marked *All Light Goes Through*, *Some Light Goes Through*, and *No Light Goes Through*.

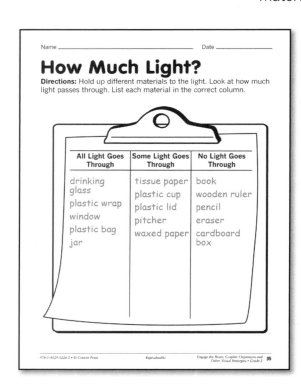

Name _____ Date _____

How Much Light?

Directions: Hold up different materials to the light. Look at how much light passes through. List each material in the correct column.

All Light Goes Through	Some Light Goes Through	No Light Goes Through
drinking glass	tissue paper	book
plastic wrap	plastic cup	wooden ruler
window	plastic lid	pencil
plastic bag	pitcher	eraser
jar	waxed paper	cardboard box

978-1-4129-5226-2 • © Corwin Press   Reproducible   Engage the Brain: Graphic Organizers and Other Visual Strategies • Grade 2   **35**

Name _____   Date _____

How Much Light?

Directions: Hold up different materials to the light. Look at how much light passes through. List each material in the correct column.

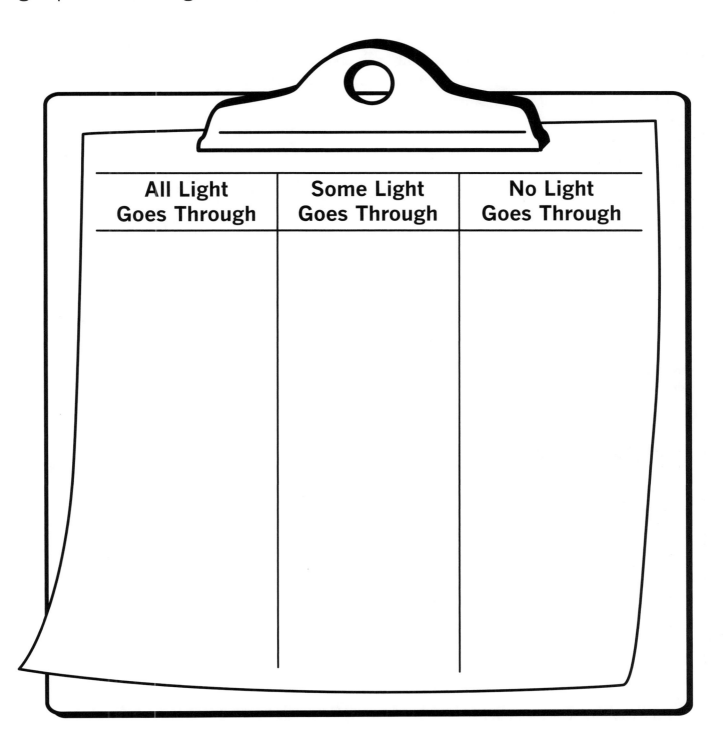

All Light Goes Through	Some Light Goes Through	No Light Goes Through

Straw Flute: Concrete Model

Materials

Straw Flute
reproducible

objects that make
sounds (e.g., 2
pencils, bell, empty
bottle, set of keys)

drinking straws

scissors

Skills Objectives

Understand that sounds change when vibrations in the air change.
Draw conclusions based on experimentation and observation.

Sounds are produced when air vibrates. Sounds change, depending
on changes in the vibrations. These concepts form the basis for how
musical instruments are produced. In this activity, students use a straw
to make a "flute" and observe how the amount of vibrating air affects
sound. The flute acts as a **Concrete Model** to demonstrate an otherwise
abstract concept.

1. Make several sounds for the class (e.g., tap two pencils together,
   ring a bell, blow across an empty bottle, jiggle a set of keys). Ask
   if students know what the sounds have in common. Explain that
   all sounds are made when the air vibrates. When these vibrations
   reach our ears, we hear sound. Tell students they will be doing an
   experiment to find out what happens when the amount of vibrating
   air changes.

2. Give each student a straw and a copy of the **Straw Flute reproducible
   (page 37)**. Read the instructions, then guide students through Step
   1 on the reproducible. Check that they bring the straw to their lips
   and blow gently. (Remind them not to touch the straw with their
   lips.) They will notice that sound is produced when they blow.

3. Have students work with partners to complete the experiment.
   Walk around the room to make sure they are conducting the
   experiment correctly.

4. Discuss questions 2 and 3 with the class. Students should have
   noticed that each time the straw was cut, the pitch got higher.

5. Discuss questions 4 and 5, and ask students why they think the
   sound changed. Guide them to see that the length of the column of
   air got shorter each time the straw was cut. The longer the column
   of air, the lower the pitch. Conversely, the shorter the column of
   air, the higher the pitch.

Extended Learning

Tell the class that woodwind instruments (such as flutes or clarinets)
make sounds when someone blows through the tube. If possible, show
a woodwind instrument to the class. Explain that a person places his
or her fingers on the instrument's holes and changes the column of air
inside the tube to make different sounds.

Name _____   Date _____

Straw Flute

Directions: Sound is produced when air vibrates. Find out what happens to the sound when you change the amount of vibrating air. Follow the steps below. Write the answers to the questions.

1. Put a straw to your lips. Blow gently across the top, without touching the straw. What happens?

_____

2. Cut off a small piece of the straw. Blow again. What happens to the sound?

_____

3. Repeat Step 2 three more times. What happens each time?

_____

_____

4. A column of air is inside the straw. What happened to the column of air each time you cut the straw?

_____

_____

5. How did the length of the column of air affect the sound?

_____

_____

Comparing Rocks: Venn Diagram

Materials

Comparing Rocks reproducible

2 large, dissimilar rocks

rock samples

magnifying glasses

tubs of water (optional)

Skills Objectives

Recognize the characteristics of rocks.
Identify similarities and differences.

Rocks have distinguishing characteristics, such as color, texture, and luster. In this activity, students study rocks and note their observations on a **Venn Diagram**. This graphic organizer allows students to organize different and shared traits.

1. Hold up two large rocks. Ask students to describe how they are alike and different.

2. Draw two large, overlapping circles on the board to make a Venn diagram. Label the left circle *Rock 1* and the right circle *Rock 2*. Ask students to call out words or phrases describing the two rocks. Write their responses in the diagram—differences in the outer parts of the circles and similarities in the overlapping part.

3. Point out that rocks have many characteristics, and list them on the board: *color, shape, texture, design* (such as stripes or speckles) and *luster* (how dull or shiny a rock is). Tell the class that scientists use these characteristics to classify or identify different kinds of rocks.

4. Give each student a magnifying glass and a copy of the **Comparing Rocks reproducible (page 39)**. Then let him or her choose two rocks to compare. Students will examine the rocks to look for characteristics listed on the board. If you wish, provide tubs of water so students can wet the rocks to see the colors better or put their rocks in the tubs to see if they float.

5. Have students write their observations on their Venn diagrams, and then share their work with a classmate.

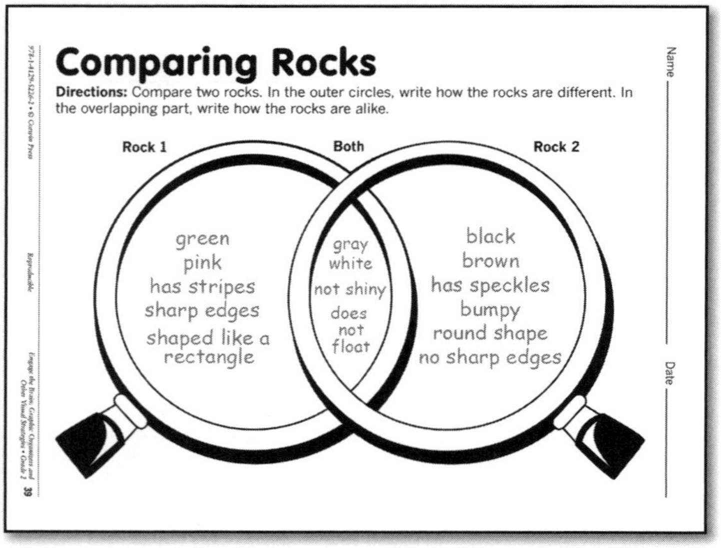

Extended Learning

Invite students to take turns sharing the information on their Venn diagrams while the rest of the class guesses which two rocks were compared.

Comparing Rocks

Directions: Compare two rocks. In the outer circles, write how the rocks are different. In the overlapping part, write how the rocks are alike.

Rock 1 — Both — Rock 2

green
pink
has stripes
sharp edges
shaped like a rectangle

gray
white
not shiny
does not float

black
brown
has speckles
bumpy
round shape
no sharp edges

Name _____ Date _____

Comparing Rocks

Directions: Compare two rocks. In the outer circles, write how the rocks are different. In the overlapping part, write how the rocks are alike.

Rock 2

Both

Rock 1

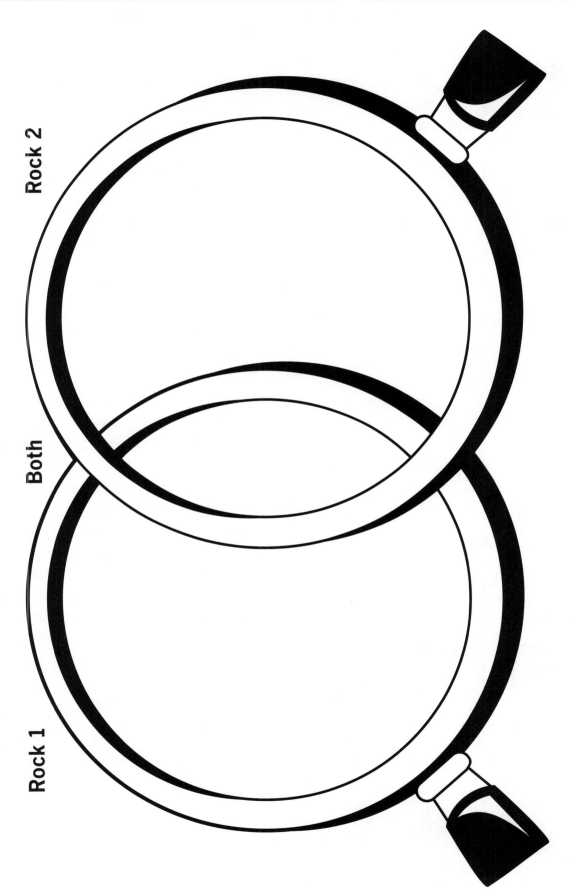

Moon Watch: Picture Chart

Materials

Moon Watch reproducible

picture of a full moon

5" Styrofoam ball

pencil

flashlight

Skills Objectives

Understand that the moon's appearance changes as it orbits Earth. Observe, identify, and record the changing shapes of the moon.

First-hand observation is an important part of scientific discovery. A **Picture Chart** is a useful way to record changes over time. In this activity, students study the moon over a period of weeks and draw their observations to make a picture chart.

1. Show the class a picture of a full moon and note its circular shape. Explain that sometimes the moon looks like a circle and sometimes it looks like a half circle or crescent, because different parts are lit as it moves around the earth.

2. Insert a pencil into a Styrofoam ball to represent a moon. Ask a student to stand in front of the room and hold the "moon." Then darken the room and stand behind the class. Shine a flashlight directly onto the ball.

3. Have the student holding the ball move slightly to the left or right. Keep the flashlight in the same position. Note that the shape of the moon no longer looks like a circle because some of it falls into darkness. As the moon travels around Earth, the sun lights different parts of it.

4. Tell students that they will observe the moon from home. Distribute copies of the **Moon Watch reproducible (page 41)**. Instruct students to look at the moon every three days and color the circles with yellow and black crayons to show what they see. Tell them to use yellow for the lit part of the moon and black for the dark part of the moon.

5. Afterwards, have students bring their pictures to school. Discuss how the moon seems to get larger or smaller as the days pass. Ask what the moon would have looked like if the class continued their observations. Guide students to see that the moon's appearance continually changes in a cycle.

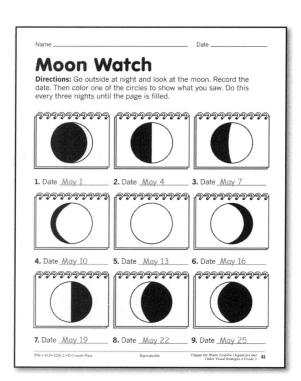

Name _____   Date _____

Moon Watch

Directions: Go outside at night and look at the moon. Record the date. Then color one of the circles to show what you saw. Do this every three nights until the page is filled.

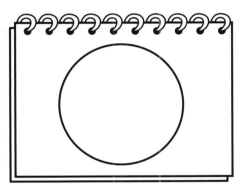 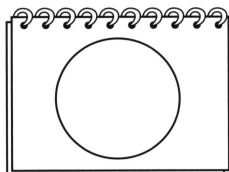 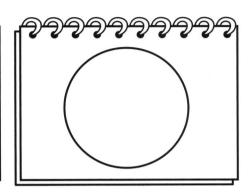

1. Date _____ **2.** Date _____ **3.** Date _____

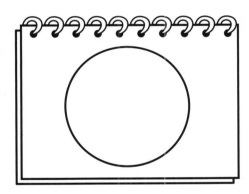 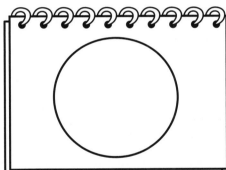 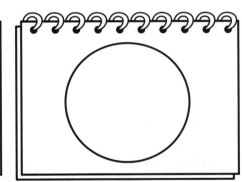

4. Date _____ **5.** Date _____ **6.** Date _____

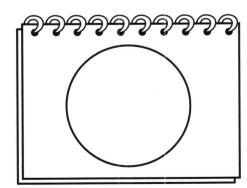 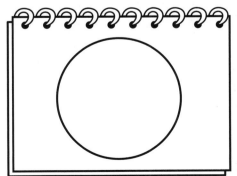 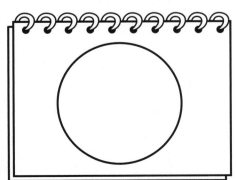

7. Date _____ **8.** Date _____ **9.** Date _____

Natural Resources: Two-Column Chart

Materials

Natural Resources
reproducible

bottle of
drinking water

small bag of soil

container of rocks

library books,
encyclopedias,
and other research
materials

Skills Objectives

Identify natural resources and the ways people use them.
Organize information on a chart.

A **Chart** allows students to organize and find information quickly and easily. In this activity, students work together to make a chart that highlights the importance of natural resources.

1. Show students a bottle of drinking water, a small bag of soil, and a container of rocks. Ask what the water, soil, and rocks have in common. *(They are all found in nature.)* Brainstorm different ways people use these materials. Explain that they are natural resources—things found in nature that meet people's needs.

2. Give students a copy of the **Natural Resources reproducible (page 43)**. Read the paragraph at the top of the page. Then work with students to complete the left side of the chart. Choose a natural resource, such as water. Title the left column *Water*. Then brainstorm different ways people use water, and write the ideas on the board. Have students fill in their charts as you write.

3. Pair up students to complete the second column. Instruct each pair to choose a natural resource and list its uses. Provide books and other resources for student research.

4. Have students share their work. Guide them to see that people and animals depend on natural resources.

Extended Learning

Have students select one resource and make a web of the different ways that resource is used. For example, a web titled *Ways We Use Water* can include: *drinking, cooking, recreation, cleaning, transportation*. Each subtopic can offer specific examples, such as *waterskiing, boating, fishing,* and *ice-skating*.

Name _____ Date _____

Natural Resources

A **natural resource** is something found in nature that people use. Air, water, rocks, plants, and soil are all natural resources. They can be used in many different ways.

Directions: Make a chart telling how people use two natural resources. Write the names of the resources at the top. Then list how each resource can be used.

Water	Plants
-drinking	-food for people and animals
-watering plants	
-boating	-trees used for lumber and paper
-water skiing	-wood used for fuel
-home for goldfish	-flowers decorate homes
-washing	-cotton used for clothes
-cleaning	-medicines come from some plants

Natural Resources

A **natural resource** is something found in nature that people use. Air, water, rocks, plants, and soil are all natural resources. They can be used in many different ways.

Directions: Make a chart telling how people use two natural resources. Write the names of the resources at the top. Then list how each resource can be used.

CHAPTER 3

Social Studies

Classroom Quilt: Picture Chart

Materials

My Family reproducible

My Family Square reproducible

personal photo album

art supplies

butcher paper

Skills Objectives

Understand that individual families have special characteristics.
Create pictures and symbols that represent one's unique background.

A **Picture Chart** can be used to tell a story using pictures. Unique illustrations feature ideas in a way words often fail to do. In this activity, students make a paper quilt celebrating their family's special qualities.

Part 1

1. Bring a family photo album to school, and share a little of your background with the class. Talk about where your family comes from, and briefly describe your cultural heritage, such as languages spoken, customs, and special traditions.

2. Tell students that every family has special qualities. They will make a large paper quilt to celebrate their families' unique characteristics.

3. Give students a copy of the **My Family reproducible (page 45)** to complete as homework. Have students ask an adult family member to help them answer the questions, and then bring their reproducibles back to school.

Part 2

1. Give students a copy of the **My Family Square reproducible (page 46)**. Invite them to draw pictures or symbols honoring their families. For example, they might draw flags of their ancestors' homeland, symbols of special holidays, words from their native language, or their family's favorite food or pastime. Students can refer to their questionnaires to help them design their squares.

2. Have students color and cut out their squares. Then glue the squares in rows on butcher paper to form the quilt. Draw "stitches" around the quilt with marker.

3. Display the quilt on a bulletin board, and invite students to talk about the pictures on their squares.

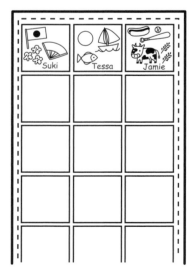

Name _____   Date _____

My Family

Directions: Ask a family member to help with the questions.

1. What part of the world does your family come from?

_____

2. When did your family first come to America?

_____

3. What kind of work did your grandparents or great-grandparents do?

_____

_____

4. How does your family enjoy spending time together?

_____

_____

_____

5. What customs or traditions does your family celebrate?

_____

_____

_____

6. What holidays, foods, and music are part of your family's culture?

_____

_____

_____

Name _____ Date _____

My Family Square

Directions: Write your name in the square. Then draw or glue pictures to honor your family. Cut out your square for the class quilt.

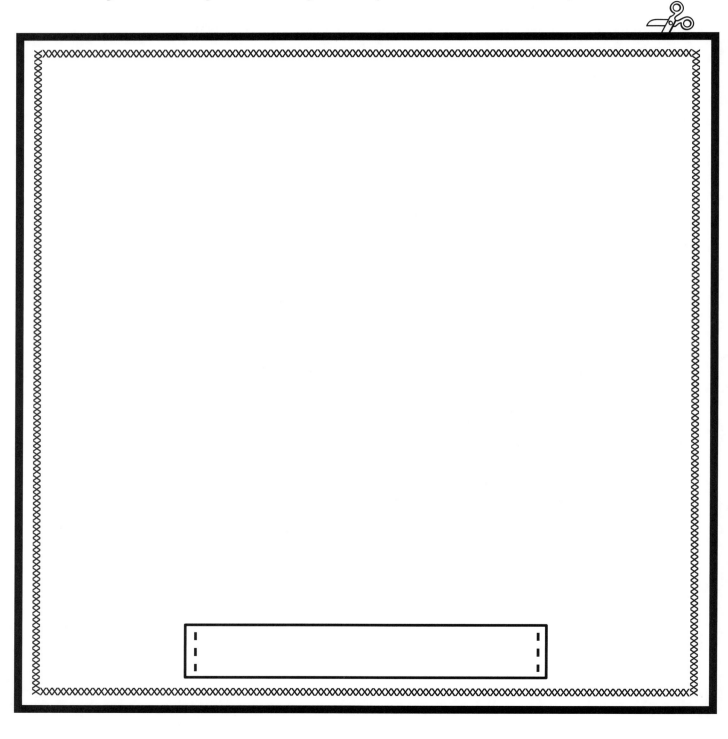

Reproducible 978-1-4129-5226-2 • © Corwin Press

Families Work Together: Two-Column Chart

Skills Objectives
Identify responsibilities of family members.
Recognize that family members need to work together.
Recognize the value of each family member.

Materials
Family Chores Chart reproducible

Students often don't realize the amount of effort that goes into running a family. By listing family chores on a chart, students can see how work is distributed among family members. A **Two-Column Chart** is an effective graphic organizer for displaying chores and the people who are responsible for them.

1. Ask students what they did to get ready for school that day. Their responses might include eating breakfast, getting dressed, and brushing their teeth. Then ask questions such as: *Who bought the food for breakfast? Who made sure you had clean clothes to wear?* Help students to see that family chores are necessary in order to keep the home running smoothly.

2. Give students a copy of the **Family Chores Chart reproducible (page 48)**. Read the first chore together (*shop for groceries*), and have students write the name of the family member who usually does that chore. Discuss responses with the class.

3. Have students continue filling in the chart. When they're done, ask the following questions to discuss the results:

   - *Which chores do only the adults in your family do?*
   - *Which chores can children do?*
   - *Does one person do most of the chores?*
   - *Are there any chores with which everyone in the family helps?*
   - *Do more children or more adults do family chores?*
   - *Can you think of other chores you can help with around the house? What are they?*

Name _____ Date _____

Family Chores Chart
Directions: Read the chart. List family members who do the chores.

Chores	Family Members Who Do the Chores
Shop for groceries	Mom, Dad
Make meals	Mom, Dad, Megan
Wash the clothes	Megan, Dad
Dust the furniture	Mom
Take out the trash	Dad, Mom, Randy
Clean the floors	Mom, Dad
Make the beds	Mom, Dad, Randy, Megan
Wash the dishes	Randy, Megan, Mom, Dad

Name _____ Date _____

Family Chores Chart

Directions: Read the chart. List family members who do the chores.

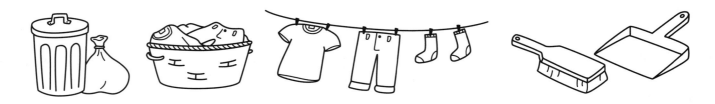

Chores	Family Members Who Do the Chores
Shop for groceries	
Make meals	
Wash the clothes	
Dust the furniture	
Take out the trash	
Clean the floors	
Make the beds	
Wash the dishes	

All Kinds of Jobs: Newspaper

Skills Objectives
Read for information.
Identify workers in a community.
Classify jobs.

Materials
All Kinds of Jobs
reproducible

newspapers

The **Newspaper** is a helpful resource for teaching a unit on community helpers. The classified ads as well as the news articles give information on many kinds of jobs. Let your class scan through the newspaper to discover the different kinds of workers needed in a community.

1. Provide newspapers for the class. (If you cannot get a set from the local newspaper, students may be able to bring in newspapers from home.) Point out the classified ads section. Tell students that the classifieds are also called the "want ads." Explain that employers use the classifieds to advertise jobs.

2. Have students look through the classifieds and the news articles for different kinds of jobs. Ask them to name the job titles they see. List the jobs on the board.

3. Tell students that jobs can be grouped according to the type of work that is done. For example, some jobs deal with construction (carpenter, architect), while others involve health care (nurse, doctor). Then distribute copies of the **All Kinds of Jobs reproducible (page 50)**.

4. Discuss the six job categories on the reproducible. Have students identify any jobs on the board that can be placed in those categories. Underline jobs related to construction in one color, jobs related to transportation in another color, and so on.

5. Divide the class into small groups. Have group members work together to fill in the charts. Students may use the jobs listed on the board, or they may come up with their own ideas. They may also design their own mini-charts for jobs that do not fit the given categories.

6. When they are finished, let the groups share their charts with the class. Initiate a discussion of what kinds of jobs students might pursue when they grow up.

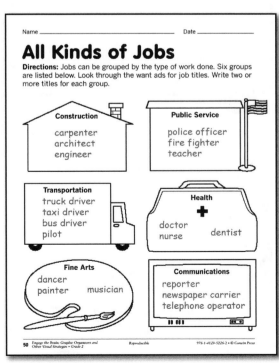

All Kinds of Jobs

Directions: Jobs can be grouped by the type of work done. Six groups are listed below. Look through the want ads for job titles. Write two or more titles for each group.

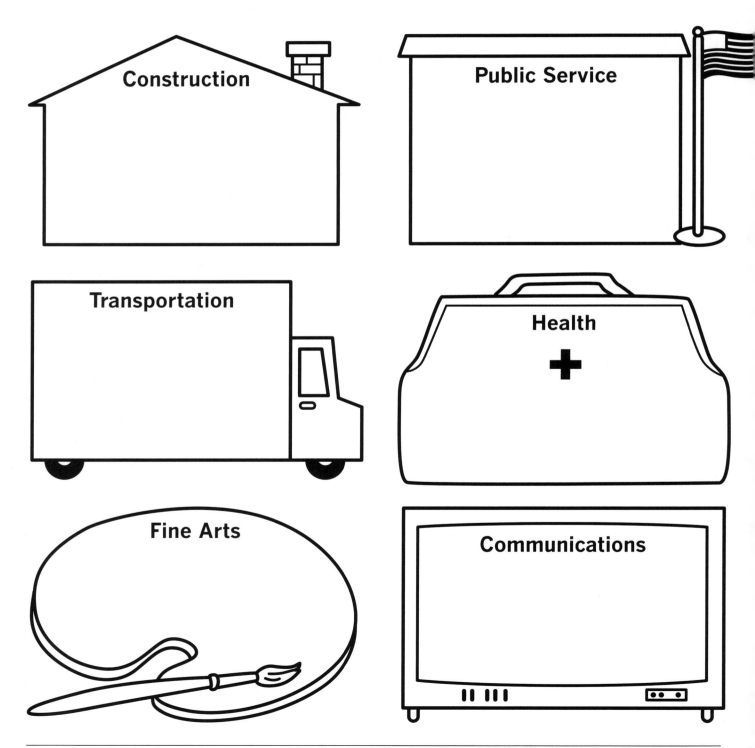

Construction

Public Service

Transportation

Health

Fine Arts

Communications

Community Helpers in My World: Idea Web

Skills Objectives

Recognize the interdependence of people in a community.
Identify community helpers.

Materials
Community Helpers reproducible

An **Idea Web** helps organize information and easily shows how words or ideas relate to each other. Students regularly come into contact with many community helpers. This activity will help them appreciate the many people in their community who have an impact on their lives.

1. Name some of the staff at your school, such as the principal, librarian, and custodian. Ask students what these workers have in common. *(They all work at your school.)* Explain that many kinds of workers are needed in a school community to keep everything running smoothly.

2. Tell students that their world is filled with community helpers, not just at school, but also at stores, libraries, hospitals, and many other places. Ask students to name community helpers they know personally or see regularly, such as a doctor, dentist, teacher, vet, and mail carrier.

3. Tell students that they will be making a web to show different community helpers in their lives. Give students a copy of the **Community Helpers reproducible (page 52)**, and have them write their name in the middle circle. Ask students to list community helpers in the connecting circles, including the names of workers they know personally. As students work, walk around the room and ask questions such as: *How does that person help you? How might your life be different if that person weren't there to help you?*

4. When students are done, ask them to share the workers they chose for their webs and explain why.

Extended Learning

Invite students to make a thank-you card for one of the community helpers they chose. Have them write why that person is important to them.

Community Helpers

Directions: Make a web showing helpers in your community. Write your name in the middle circle. Then write a community worker in each outer circle. Write the worker's name if you know it.

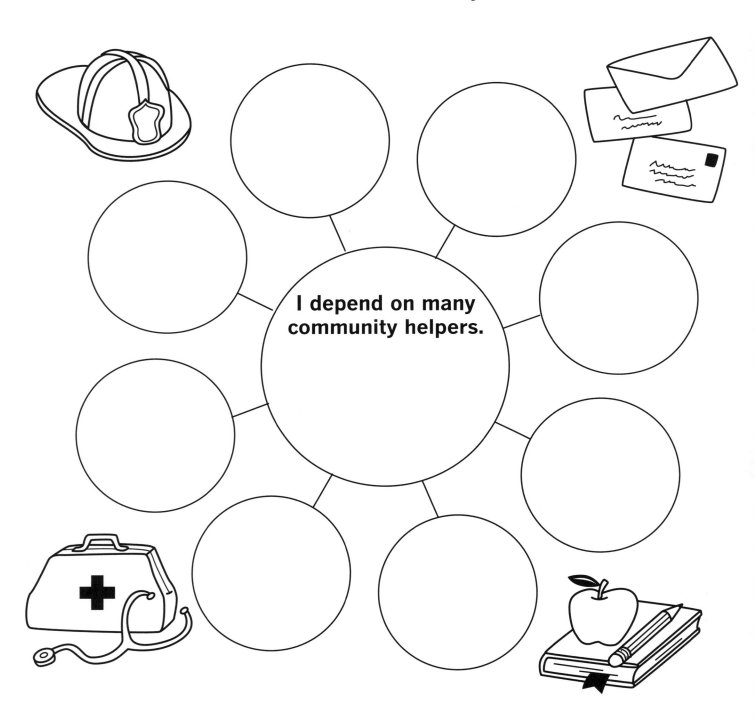

My Different Communities: Graphic Model

Skills Objectives

Identify different communities to which a person belongs.
Recognize that small, nuclear communities are part of larger ones.

Materials

I Belong to Communities reproducible

6 colors of butcher paper

scissors

markers

glue

Primary students often have difficulty understanding what actually makes up a community. Introduce a **Graphic Model** to help students understand that they belong to different communities, beginning with their immediate family and ending with the world at large.

1. Cut different-sized circles from six colors of butcher paper. The smallest circle should be no smaller than eight inches across.

2. Glue the circles one on top of the other in order of size until you have a large circle that resembles a target.

3. Display your model for the class. Explain that each circle stands for a certain kind of community. Tell students that they belong to each of these communities.

4. Write *family* in the smallest circle. Tell students that they are each part of a family. Add that the family name, such as *Lee* or *Gonzalez*, identifies the family community.

5. Write *neighborhood* in the second smallest circle. Tell students that they also belong to a neighborhood. Add that their street name identifies this community.

6. Write *city* (or *town*) in the third circle. Tell students that they are also part of a larger community called a city. Invite students to say the name of their city.

7. Write *state* in the fourth circle. Tell students that they are also part of a state. Explain that a state is made up of many cities and their surrounding areas. Then have students say the name of their state.

8. Write *country* in the fifth circle. Tell students that they belong to a very large community called a country. Explain that their country is made up of 50 states. Then have students say the name of their country. *(United States of America)*

9. Finally, write *world* in the sixth circle. Tell students that this is the largest community of all. Have them say the name of this community. *(Earth)* Explain that everyone belongs to this community.

10. Inform students that each smaller circle is part of the larger circles surrounding it. In the same way, communities are part of larger ones. Give students a copy of the **I Belong to Communities reproducible (page 55)**.

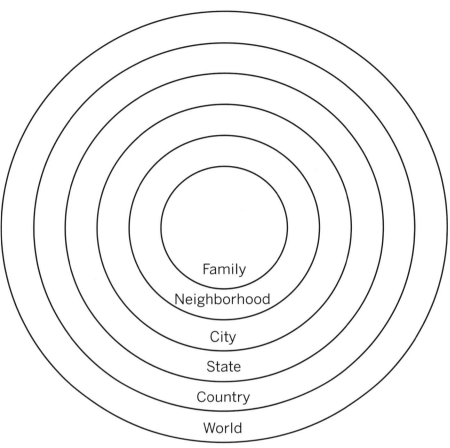

Family
Neighborhood
City
State
Country
World

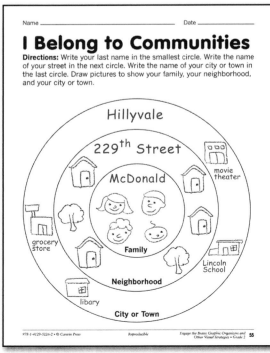

11. Point to the smallest circle in the middle of the page. Tell students that this circle represents their family community. Have them write their family name in the circle. Next, have students write their street name on the next circle to identify their neighborhood and write their city or town name in the last circle.

12. Invite students to complete the page by drawing pictures inside the circles. For example, students might draw family members in the center circle, houses and trees in the middle circle, and buildings (such as a school and hospital) in the outer circle. Tell students to label the pictures in the outer circle.

13. Display students' work on a bulletin board titled *My Different Communities.*

I Belong to Communities

Directions: Write your last name in the smallest circle. Write the name of your street in the next circle. Write the name of your city or town in the last circle. Draw pictures to show your family, your neighborhood, and your city or town.

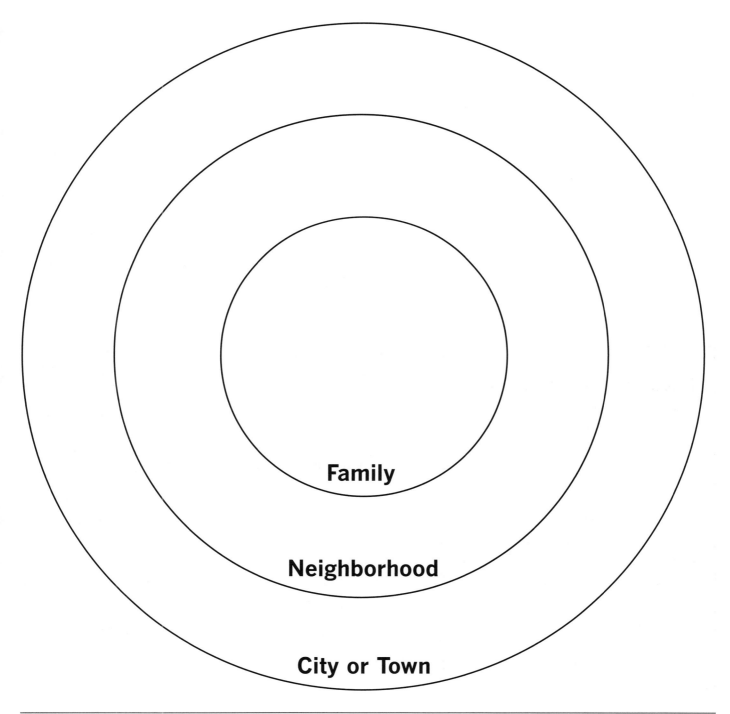

Family

Neighborhood

City or Town

Filmstrip Timeline

Materials

Filmstrip Timeline reproducible

children's resources about famous people (biographies, encyclopedias)

Skills Objectives

Research information about a person.
Identify main events in a person's life and put them in sequential order.

A **Timeline** presents events in chronological order on a linear model so the sequence of events is clear. Identifying main events and sequential order are important skills. In this activity, students research famous people and present facts about their lives on a timeline.

Part 1

1. Show students biographies and encyclopedia articles that tell about interesting and important people. Help students see that biographies are often written in "time order," or chronologically.

2. Tell students they will be researching and writing about famous people. Provide books and other resources. Let students look through the materials and choose a person to research.

Part 2

1. As students research, have them list important dates and events from their person's life. Remind them to choose events that will help others understand who that person is and why he or she is important. Make sure students select appropriate events.

2. Have students circle the four most important events on their list. Then give them a copy of the **Filmstrip Timeline reproducible (page 57)**. Tell students to write the name of their person at the top and list the dates of four events in order. Finally, have them briefly describe and illustrate the events.

3. Invite students to present their timelines to the class.

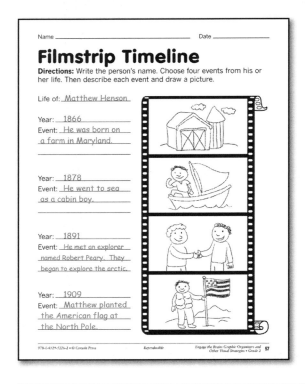

Filmstrip Timeline

Directions: Write the person's name. Choose four events from his or her life. Then describe each event and draw a picture.

Life of: _____

Year: _____
Event: _____
_____
_____

Year: _____
Event: _____
_____
_____

Year: _____
Event: _____
_____
_____

Year: _____
Event: _____
_____
_____

The Bread Trail: Flowchart

Skills Objectives

Read for information.

Identify and summarize the steps in a process.

List information sequentially.

<table>
<tr><td>

Materials

How We Get Bread reproducible

The Bread Trail reproducible

loaf of bread

</td></tr>
</table>

A **Flowchart** shows a series of steps in a complex process. In this activity, students read about how bread is made from wheat. Then they use a flowchart to outline the process.

1. Show students a loaf of bread, and ask the class where it came from. Explain that many things had to happen in order to get the bread to the store.

2. Give students a copy of the **How We Get Bread reproducible (page 59)**, and read the story together. Discuss the places wheat must go so bread can get to the store.

3. Ask students to identify the seven places that are part of the bread trail. *(farm, country elevator, terminal elevator, flour mill, bakery, warehouse, supermarket)* Have them underline these places in the story.

4. Give students a copy of **The Bread Trail reproducible (page 60)**. Point out the boxes and arrows. Discuss how the arrows lead from one box to the next. Tell students they can use the flowchart to show how bread gets to the supermarket.

5. Have students refer to the story and the underlined words. Ask them to name the first place on the bread trail *(farm)* and explain what happens there. *(Farmers plant, grow, and harvest wheat.)* Have students fill in all the boxes in the flowchart.

6. When they are done, initiate a discussion about where other items come from, such as cotton for clothing, oranges for orange juice, or milk for cereal or cookies.

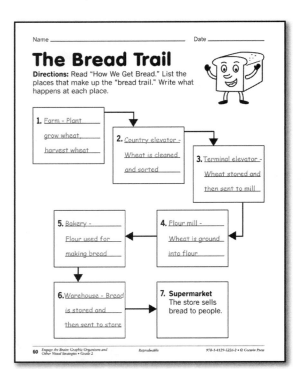

Name _____ Date _____

How We Get Bread

Directions: Read the story and find out how bread gets to the grocery store. Underline the seven places on the "bread trail." Then write them on the lines below.

Where do you get a loaf of bread? Many people get their bread from a supermarket. But how did the bread get to the store in the first place?

The "bread trail" begins at a farm. Bread is made from flour, and flour comes from wheat. Farmers plant, grow, and harvest the wheat. Then they transport it by truck to a large building called a country grain elevator. This elevator cleans and sorts the wheat.

The country grain elevator sends the wheat to a terminal elevator. The wheat is stored there until it is time for shipping. When the wheat is ready to be made into flour, it goes to a mill. The mill grinds the wheat into a fine powder called flour. The mill ships the flour to a bakery where bread is made.

Next, the bread is sent to a large building called a warehouse. The warehouse stores the bread until it is time to send it to the supermarket. There the bread trail ends. The supermarket then sells bread to people like you and me!

1. _____ 2. _____

3. _____ 4. _____

5. _____ 6. _____

7. _____

Name _____   Date _____

The Bread Trail

Directions: Read "How We Get Bread." List the places that make up the "bread trail." Write what happens at each place.

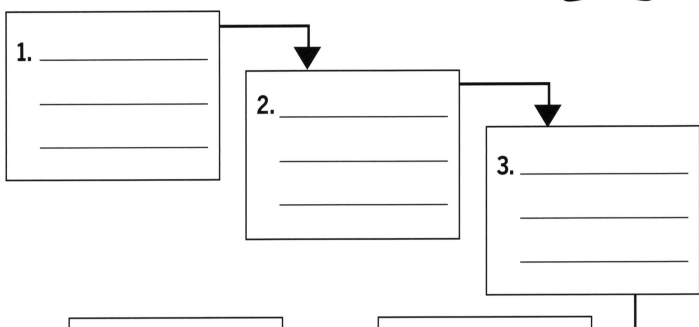

1. _____ _____ _____

2. _____ _____ _____

3. _____ _____ _____

5. _____ _____ _____

4. _____ _____ _____

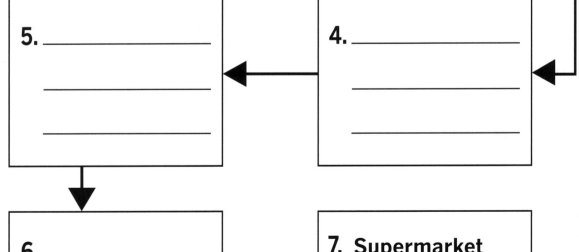

6. _____ _____ _____

7. **Supermarket**
The store sells bread to people.

One Country, Many Citizens: Collage

Skills Objectives
Recognize that many different people make up the United States.
Recognize that all citizens, regardless of background, share similar
dreams and goals.

Materials
One Country, Many
Citizens reproducible

United States map

magazines

scissors

glue

A **Collage** juxtaposes different images into a cohesive whole. The
United States is one of the largest countries in the world, with one of the
most diverse populations. Let students celebrate America's diversity by
making a collage featuring citizens from all backgrounds.

1. Display a map of the United States. Explain that millions of people
   live in our country. A country is made up of *citizens*. A citizen is
   someone who belongs to a country. Elicit from students that a
   United States citizen is called an *American*.

2. Ask students what an American looks like. Guide them to see that
   Americans come from many different cultures and ethnic groups.
   People from all over the world make America their home.

3. Ask students how Americans are alike. Help them see that
   although American citizens may look different from one another,
   they share common dreams and goals. Brainstorm with students
   what these dreams and goals might be (e.g., *go to college, get a
   good job, provide a home for their families, make America a safe
   place to live*).

4. Invite students to make a colorful collage celebrating America's
   diversity. Give each student an enlarged copy of the **One Country,
   Many Citizens reproducible (page 62)**. Tell students to cut out magazine
   pictures of people who represent American citizens, and glue
   the pictures on their maps, keeping inside the outline as much
   as possible. Urge them to
   overlap pictures so white
   spaces are kept to
   a minimum.

5. Post collages on a bulletin
   board for an eye-catching,
   patriotic display.

One Country, Many Citizens

Directions: Cut out pictures of people who look like American citizens. Glue them to the map to make a collage.

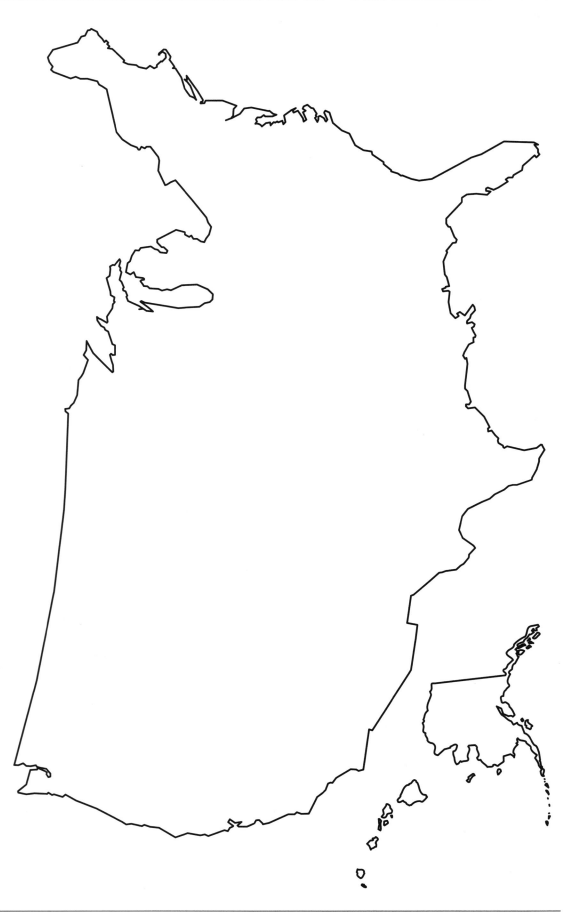

Engage the Brain: Graphic Organizers and Other Visual Strategies • Grade 2   *Reproducible*   978-1-4129-5226-2 • © Corwin Press

CHAPTER 4

Language Arts

Character Balloons: Venn Diagram

Skills Objectives
Recognize character traits.
Distinguish between similarities and differences.

Materials
Character Balloons
reproducible

A **Venn Diagram** helps students visualize similarities and differences, and is a useful tool for making comparisons. In this activity, students use a Venn diagram to compare and contrast two fictional characters.

1. Ask students to name the characters in a book they're reading. List the characters on the board. Together, choose two characters to compare and contrast. For example, if students are reading *Miss Nelson Is Missing!* by James Marshall, let them compare the teachers *Miss Nelson* and *Miss Swamp*.

2. Draw two large, overlapping circles on the board to make a Venn diagram. Write a character's name at the top of each circle, and have students tell one way the characters are different. Write the traits in the outer parts of the circles. For example, write *blond hair* under Miss Nelson and *black hair* under Miss Swamp.

3. Have students tell one way the characters are alike. Write that trait in the overlapping section of the diagram.

4. Give students a copy of the **Character Balloons reproducible (page 64)**. They can create a Venn diagram for two characters, referring to the diagram on the board. When comparing, they should think of personality, circumstances, and physical traits. Remind students to list differences in the outer parts of the balloons and similarities in the overlapping part.

5. Check students' ideas as they work. If students have difficulty thinking of words or phrases, ask leading questions such as: *Would you like that character for a friend? Why or why not?* Afterward, allow students to compare their diagrams.

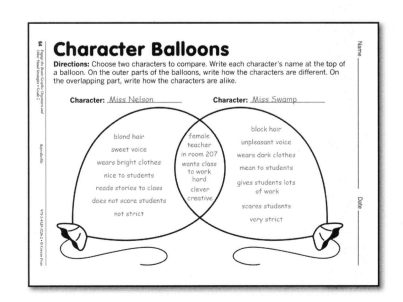

Character Balloons

Directions: Choose two characters to compare. Write each character's name at the top of a balloon. On the outer parts of the balloons, write how the characters are different. On the overlapping part, write how the characters are alike.

Character: _____

Character: _____

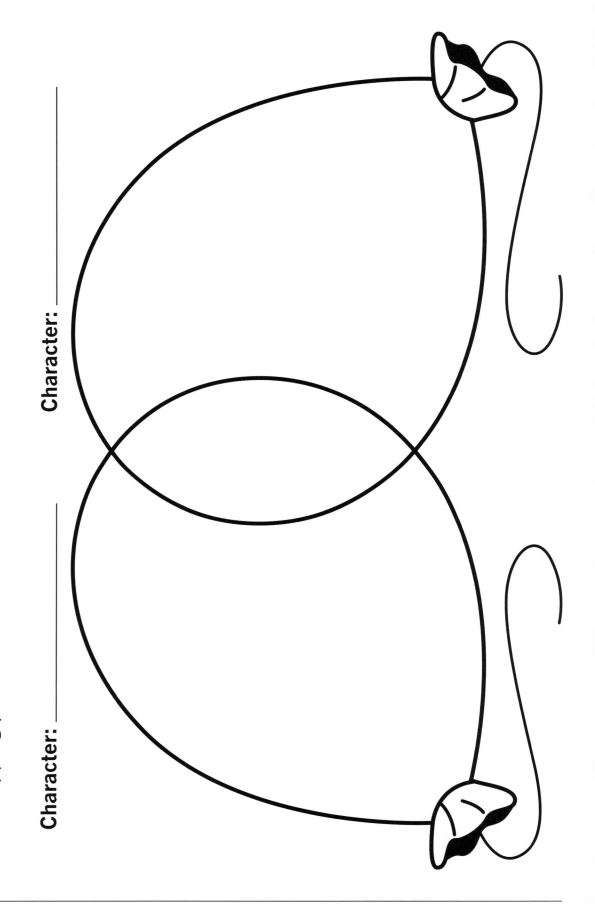

Hop to It! Chain of Events Map

Skills Objectives
Identify main events in a story.
Sequence events in a story.

Materials
Hop to It! reproducible

paper chain

A **Chain of Events Map** helps students display information that needs to be arranged in chronological order. The individual "links" are connected so the sequence of events is clearly visible. This activity gives students practice in exploring plot structure. Do the activity after the class has read a story together.

1. Hold up a paper chain made of several links. Point out that each link is connected to another to form the chain. Tell students they will create a chain of events based on a story they've read. The chain will be made of the story's main events.

2. Brainstorm several events from the story. Write them on the board. Then have students vote on the five most important events, and circle the "winners." For example, if students are reading *The Bremen Town Musicians*, they might start with the sentence *A donkey, dog, cat, and rooster leave for Bremen Town*, and end with *The animals stay in the house and never go to Bremen Town.*

3. Distribute copies of the **Hop to It! reproducible (page 66)**. Point out the "chain" of lily pads. Point out how each lily pad is connected to the next one. Instruct students to write the title of the story, and then the story's five main events in order on the lily pads.

4. When they're done, invite volunteers to read their five events aloud. Discuss that when a story's main events are read (or written) in order, they give a summary—a short version of the story.

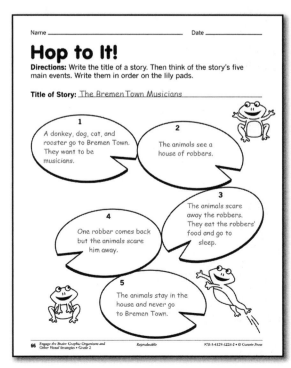

Hop to It!

Directions: Write the title of a story. Then think of the story's five main events. Write them in order on the lily pads.

Title of Story: _____

Pyramid of Facts: Pyramid Chart

Skills Objectives
Determine the main idea or topic of a book.
Recall details and communicate facts.

Materials
Pyramid of Facts
reproducible

crayons or markers

scissors

A **Pyramid Chart** divided into layers provides a visual tool for presenting simple, abbreviated facts. In this activity, students use a pyramid chart to record information learned from a nonfiction book they've read.

1. Review with students the difference between fiction and nonfiction. Remind them that nonfiction books are true and provide facts and information. Invite volunteers to name nonfiction books they've read. Ask students why they chose these books. Help them to see that people read nonfiction books for interest and to get information.

2. Tell students that they will present what they learn using a special pyramid. Give them a copy of the **Pyramid of Facts reproducible (page 68)**. Read the five sections of the pyramid. Check that students understand how to complete the chart by having them state sample answers for each section.

3. Invite students to complete each section of their chart, recording facts about a nonfiction book they have read or are currently reading. Be available if students need assistance or have questions.

4. When they're finished, have students color and cut out their pyramids. Display the pyramids on a bulletin board titled *Our Pyramids of Facts.*

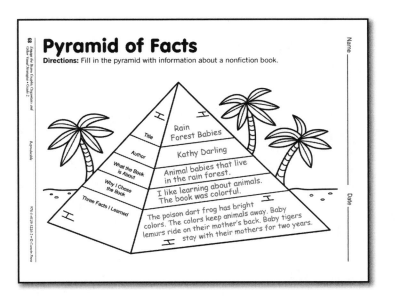

Pyramid of Facts

Directions: Fill in the pyramid with information about a nonfiction book.

Title

Author

What the Book is About

Why I Chose the Book

Three Facts I Learned

Engage the Brain: Graphic Organizers and Other Visual Strategies • Grade 2 *Reproducible* 978-1-4129-5226-2 • © Corwin Press

Stand-Up Book Report: Three-Dimensional Display

Skills Objectives
Identify story elements.
Communicate information about a book.
Create a three-dimensional display.

Materials
Stand-Up Book Report reproducible

construction paper

heavy paper

scissors

glue

A **Three-Dimensional Display** adds an interesting twist to an otherwise ordinary book report. In this activity, students make a stand-up display that highlights the major elements of a story. Do the activity after your class has already been introduced to the following concepts: setting, character, problem, and solution.

1. Tell students that they will be making a special book report in class. Copy the **Stand-Up Book Report reproducible (page 70)** on heavy paper and distribute to students. Review the following terms:

   - Setting—when and where the story takes place
   - Characters—who the story is about
   - Problem—the difficulty or concern the main character faces
   - Solution—how the problem is solved

2. Review the terms by discussing a book the class has read together. Have students name the setting and main character(s), state the problem, and describe how the problem was resolved.

3. Have students use the Stand-Up Book Report reproducible to write about a book of their choice. Instruct them to write the title and author's name in the bottom two boxes. They should also write about the setting, main character, problem, and solution. Invite them to add pictures if they wish. As students work, circulate around the room to make sure they understand each story element.

4. Tell students to cut out the boxes and fold up along the dotted lines. Then have them glue their boxes to a sheet of construction paper so the boxes stand up.

5. Display book reports along a shelf, so students can read them in their spare time.

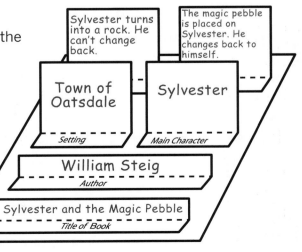

Stand-Up Book Report

Directions: Fill in each box. Add pictures if you wish. Then cut out the boxes along the solid lines. Fold up along the dotted lines to make tabs. Glue the tabs to a sheet of construction paper.

Setting	**Main Character**
Problem	**Solution**

Title of Book

Author

Zoom in on the Main Idea: E-Chart

Skills Objectives
Identify the main idea and supporting details in a passage.
Write a paragraph that has a clear main idea and supporting details.

Materials
Zoom in on the Main Idea reproducible

chart paper

An **E-Chart** links a topic or theme with three supporting ideas. An E-chart resembles the shape of a capital *E*, with the middle stem extended to the left. An E-chart is an effective prewriting tool. Students can write a main idea on the long stem of the *E*. Then they can list supporting details on the three short stems. Students can refer to their chart when they are ready to do a writing assignment.

1. Ahead of time, copy the following passage on a sheet of chart paper: *Did you know that a peanut is more than just a tasty snack? A peanut has many uses. It is a main ingredient of peanut butter and cooking oil. It is also used for making soap, shampoo, and paint. In fact, an American scientist named George Washington Carver found over 300 uses for the peanut plant!*

2. Read the passage with the class. Guide students in finding the main idea, and underline it on the chart. *(A peanut has many uses.)* Then have students read the passage again. Ask them to state the details that support the main idea. Underline these phrases or sentences on the chart. *(It is a main ingredient of peanut butter and cooking oil; it is also used for making soap, shampoo, and paint; over 300 uses for the peanut plant.)*

3. Inform students that the main idea is the main topic, or focus, of the writing. Details are pieces of information that explain or defend the main idea. Tell students that all details in their writing should connect to the main idea.

4. Draw a large *E* on the board, extending the middle stem to the left. Tell students that an E-chart can be used to show a main idea and supporting details. Demonstrate by using the peanut story. Write the main idea on the left side of the long stem. Then have students help you write the three details on the short stems.

A peanut has many uses | main ingredient of peanut butter and cooking oil

used for making soap, shampoo, paint

over 300 uses

5. Work as a class to write a paragraph, using an E-chart to record the main idea and details. Begin by writing the following topics on the board, and let the class choose one to write about:

- *A dog (or cat) makes a terrific pet.*
- *Watching TV can be good for you.*
- *Students should volunteer in their community.*

6. Draw an E-chart on the board. Write the main idea on the long stem. Then have students suggest three supporting details, and write them on the short stems. For example, for "a dog makes a terrific pet," students might suggest:

- *A dog is fun. It plays with you.*
- *A dog is loving. It gets excited when you come home.*
- *A dog is loyal. It protects you from danger.*

7. Next, help students combine the main idea and details to make a cohesive paragraph. Write the paragraph on the board. For example:

   Dogs make terrific pets. A dog is fun to have around because it always wants to play. You can play fetch and other games. A dog is full of love, too. It wags its tail when it's excited to see you. A dog is also loyal. It can protect you if someone tries to break into your house. There is no better pet than a dog!

8. Encourage students to use an E-chart to plan other writing assignments. Give students a copy of the **Zoom in on the Main Idea reproducible (page 73)**. Let them choose a topic, and then write the main idea and three supporting details on the chart. Have students use the ideas on their chart to write the final paragraph.

9. Students can share their paragraphs in small groups.

Name _____ Date _____

Zoom in on the Main Idea

Directions: Choose a topic to write about. Write the main idea on the racecar. Then write three details that support your main idea in the smoke clouds.

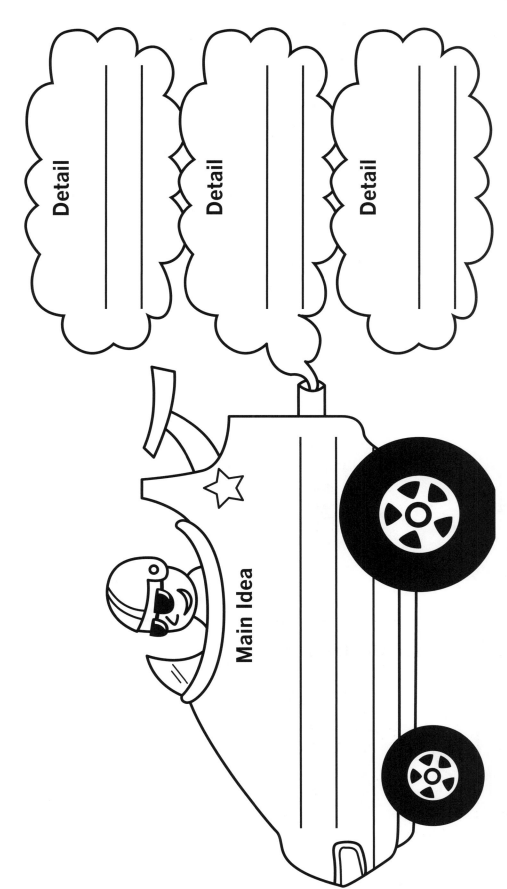

Detail

Detail

Detail

Main Idea

On another sheet of paper, write a paragraph about your topic. Use your main idea and details to help you.

Plural Garden: Word Web

Materials

Plural Flowers reproducible

crayons or colored pencils

scissors

glue

green paper

Skills Objectives

Recognize different kinds of plural endings.

Identify plural nouns that have the same ending.

Know the rules for forming plurals.

After students learn how to form various plurals, let them help you make a colorful reference chart of "plural flowers." Each flower is actually a mini graphic organizer—a **Word Web** that features the plural ending in the center, with examples of plural words on the petals.

1. Tell students that they will help you "plant" a special garden. The garden will be made from different types of plurals they have learned.

2. Give students a copy of the **Plural Flowers reproducible (page 75)**. Point out the plural ending in the center of each flower. Have students give you examples of plurals that end in -s, -es, -ies, and -ves. Write their suggestions on the board, such as: *boats, cats; foxes, peaches; pennies, babies; wolves, shelves.*

3. Have students work alone or with partners to write plurals on each flower's petals. Walk around the room to make sure students are forming plurals correctly.

4. Instruct students to lightly color their flowers and cut them out. They can then glue on stems and leaves cut from green paper.

5. Arrange the flowers on a bulletin board titled *Our Plurals Garden.*

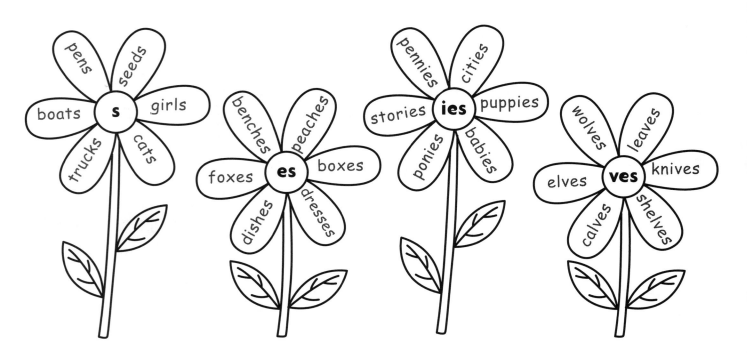

Name _____ Date _____

Plural Flowers

Directions: Look at the plural ending in the center of each flower. On the petals, write plural words with that ending.

Vowel Sounds: Collage

Materials

red and blue butcher paper

sources for pictures and words (magazines, newspapers, rubber stamps, stickers)

scissors

markers

glue

Skills Objectives

Distinguish between short and long vowel sounds.
Read and write words containing short and long vowels.

Hands-on, concrete experiences help reinforce concepts, even in those areas that traditionally focus on oral and auditory skills. A **Collage** is a visual tool that proves useful in helping students to see the relationships between various vowel sounds. In this activity, students work in groups to make collages that display their knowledge of vowel sounds. The collages provide a fun, interesting way for students to apply what they've learned.

1. For a quick vowel review, play "Sit or Stand." Say aloud short and long vowel words (e.g., *cup, bag, make, ride, team, box*). Tell students to sit if the word contains a short vowel and stand if the word has a long vowel. As you play, check that students are distinguishing vowel sounds correctly.

2. Tell students they will make collages to show the different vowel sounds they learned. Cut one set of vowels (*A, E, I, O, U*) from red butcher paper and another set from blue butcher paper. Make the letters wide and at least two feet tall.

3. Tell students that the red vowels will be short, and the blue vowels will be long. Then divide the class into five groups, and assign each group one vowel. (Each group will be responsible for both the short and long sounds of that vowel.)

4. Set out magazines, newspapers, rubber stamps, and stickers for the class. Then instruct students to look for words and pictures that have their assigned vowel sounds. Have them glue the items to their letters, and label each picture.

5. Display the collages around the room for the whole class to enjoy. Use your vowel displays to "read the room" together!

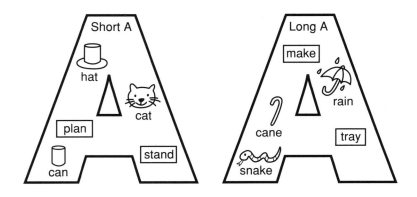

Contraction Caterpillars: Paper Model

Skills Objectives
Read and write contractions.
Identify a contraction, given the two words that form it.

Materials
Contraction
Caterpillars
reproducible

scissors

highlighters
or markers

Paper Models are fun visual aids that motivate student interest and understanding, and foster a love of learning. In this review activity, students make paper models for contractions formed with *is*, *are*, and *am*. This model will show how a letter "disappears" when two words become a contraction.

1. In advance, cut out and fold the "it is" caterpillar from the **Contraction Caterpillars reproducible (page 78)**.

2. Review with students what they know about contractions. A contraction is a shortened form of two words. Write the following sentence on the board: *I think it is going to rain.* Underline *it is*. Ask a volunteer to change the two words to a contraction, and read the sentence aloud.

3. Discuss what happened to *it is* when it became a contraction (drop the letter *i* in *is*, and put an apostrophe in its place). Write *he is* and *she is* on the board, and have volunteers write the corresponding contractions. Repeat the activity with *you are*, *they are*, *we are*, and *I am*. Point out that in these words, the *a* is dropped.

4. Next, tell students that they will make caterpillar models to remind them how contractions are formed. Hold up your paper caterpillar so that *it is* appears. Fold on the dotted line to change the two words into *it's*. Point out that the letter *i* "disappears."

5. Give students a copy of the Contraction Caterpillars reproducible. Have them color the caterpillars with highlighters or light-colored markers before cutting them out. Show the class how to fold the caterpillars to form contractions.

6. Ask students to turn over each caterpillar and write a sentence with the corresponding contraction. Later, let students read their sentences to a partner.

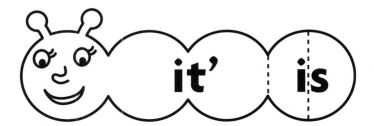 

Contraction Caterpillars

Directions: Cut out each caterpillar. Fold on the dotted lines to make the contraction. Then write a sentence with the contraction on the back of the caterpillar.

ABC Cards: Word Cards

Skills Objectives
Arrange words in alphabetical order.
Identify ways people use alphabetical order.

Materials

ABC Shopping Time reproducible

26 index cards

red and black markers

alphabet chart

Word Cards allow students to move and rearrange words, making the alphabetizing process easier to conceptualize. When introducing alphabetizing skills, provide word cards for students to manipulate. Give an extra visual clue by making the initial letter of each word a different color. Students can then focus on the part of the word that will let them alphabetize successfully.

1. Ahead of time, make a set of 26 word cards, each word beginning with a different letter of the alphabet. Use red marker to write the initial letters and black marker to write the rest of the letters. Shuffle the cards.

2. Stand next to an alphabet chart. (If you do not have one, write the alphabet on a sheet of butcher paper. Then tape it to a wall.)

3. Ask students to describe the order of words that appear in a dictionary, encyclopedia, or thesaurus. (Words beginning with *a* are first, words beginning with *b* are next, and so on.) Explain that the words are in *alphabetical order*.

4. Let students practice putting words in alphabetical order. Place four word cards along the ledge of the board. Read the words together, and have students state the initial letters. Then ask a volunteer to arrange the words in alphabetical order. Let him or her refer to the alphabet chart as needed. Afterward, have the class check the order.

5. Continue the procedure with a new student and four different word cards. Repeat the activity several times.

6. Reinforce the concept by asking students to complete the **ABC Shopping Time reproducible (page 80)**. If students have trouble alphabetizing the words, cover all but the initial letter of each word with a self-stick note. They can then arrange the initial letters in order.

Extended Learning
Teach students the value of alphabetizing by having them list the ways alphabetical order is used (e.g., *list words in dictionaries, encyclopedias, phone books, and indexes; organize books on a library shelf, files in a filing cabinet, or documents in a computer*).

ABC Shopping Time

Directions: Write each shopping list in alphabetical order. Use the alphabet chart to help you.

a b c d e f g h i j k l m n o p q r s t u v w x y z

milk
eggs
butter
ham

1. _____
2. _____
3. _____
4. _____

peas
jam
apples
cheese

1. _____
2. _____
3. _____
4. _____

tuna
grapes
muffins
juice

1. _____
2. _____
3. _____
4. _____

corn
napkins
beans
tea

1. _____
2. _____
3. _____
4. _____

plums
bread
chicken
lettuce

1. _____
2. _____
3. _____
4. _____

rice
soap
ketchup
oranges

1. _____
2. _____
3. _____
4. _____

CHAPTER 5

Physical Education, Art, and Music

Staying Fit: Picture Chart

Skills Objectives
Identify activities that foster physical fitness.
Write physical activities that one enjoys regularly.

A **Picture Chart** can help motivate students to be more active as they track their physical activity. Physical activity should be a part of every person's day to ensure overall health. Help students see that physical activity doesn't have to be in the form of sports or exercise. Any activity that gets the body moving—including walking the dog or biking to the store—can help them stay physically fit.

1. Ask students why they think recess is an important part of the school day. (If possible, ask this question just after the recess or when lunchtime is over.) Tell the class that recess not only breaks up the day, but it also gives students a chance to get some physical activity.

2. Talk about the kinds of things students can do to be active. Write suggestions on the board. The class probably will mention sports and exercise. Tell students that sports and exercise are great for promoting physical fitness, but less rigorous forms of activity are just as helpful. Vacuuming the house, mowing the lawn, playing tag, and walking to the park are all forms of physical activity. Tell students it is important that they spend time doing some form of physical activity every day.

3. Give students a copy of the **I Can Stay Fit! reproducible (page 82)**, and tell them to draw a picture of themselves on the kite. On each bow of the kite's tail, have students list a physical activity they enjoy. Remind them that not every activity has to involve sports or exercise.

4. Have students finish the page by coloring the picture. Then pair up students and have partners brainstorm more ways they can stay fit, both at school and at home.

Materials
I Can Stay Fit!
Reproducible

crayons or markers

Name _____ Date _____

I Can Stay Fit!
Directions: Draw a picture of yourself on the kite. Then think of physical activities you enjoy. List them on the bows of the kite's tail. Color your picture.

play tag play soccer swim walk my dog play at park ride bike

82 *Engage the Brain: Graphic Organizers and Other Visual Strategies • Grade 2*   Reproducible   978-1-4129-5226-2 • © Corwin Press

I Can Stay Fit!

Directions: Draw a picture of yourself on the kite. Then think of physical activities you enjoy. List them on the bows of the kite's tail. Color your picture.

Staying Fit All Year: Matrix

Skills Objectives
Identify physical activities done throughout the year.
Evaluate one's own activity routines.

Materials
Staying Fit All Year reproducible

A **Matrix** can help students evaluate how active they are during different times of the year. In this activity, students make a matrix displaying the kinds of physical activities they do throughout the year. If possible, do the following activity after your class has completed the "Staying Fit" activity on page 81.

1. Ask students to share the kinds of physical activities they like to do throughout the year. Have them include activities that are specific to a season, such as ice-skating (winter) or swimming (summer). Write their responses on the board.

2. Ask students to predict in which season they are the most active. Then pass out copies of the **Staying Fit All Year reproducible (page 84)**. Tell students to list their six favorite physical activities down the left side of the matrix.

3. Next, have students look at their first activity and determine in which season(s) they do that activity. Tell them to check off the boxes under the appropriate seasons. Then have them repeat the procedure for the remaining activities.

4. When students have completed their matrices, have them look at the pattern of checkmarks and answer the following questions:

   - *Which activities do you do only during one season?*
   - *Which activities do you do for most of the year?*
   - *In which season are you the most active? How do you know?*
   - *What other activities could you add to the list to keep more active?*

Name _____ Date _____

Staying Fit All Year
Directions: List six activities you enjoy that help you stay fit. List them down the left side of the chart. Then check off the boxes to show which season you do each activity.

	Spring	Summer	Fall	Winter
playing tag	✓	✓	✓	
swimming		✓		
ice skating				✓
riding bike	✓	✓	✓	
walking the dog	✓	✓	✓	✓
soccer	✓	✓	✓	

84 *Engage the Brain: Graphic Organizers and Other Visual Strategies • Grade 2*   *Reproducible*   978-1-4129-5226-2 • © Corwin Press

Staying Fit All Year

Directions: List six activities you enjoy that help you stay fit. List them down the left side of the chart. Then check off the boxes to show which season you do each activity.

	Spring	Summer	Fall	Winter

Colors Help Us See: Graphic Chart

Skills Objectives
Understand that colors help us perceive things around us.
Recognize that colors can be grouped by characteristics.
Identify like colors and group them accordingly.

Graphic Charts can be used to help group objects by categories, including colors. Color adds interest and beauty to our world. It enhances our perceptions and makes our view more pleasurable. Help students understand the importance of color and its many variations by doing the following activity.

1. In advance, make a black-and-white photocopy of a color illustration from a magazine. Show the photocopy to the class, and ask students what they see. Ask questions such as: *What color is the boy's shirt? Can you tell the color of the house? What is the dark object behind the tree?*

2. Ask students to guess how many colors are actually in the picture. Then show the color picture for comparison. Discuss the fact that color not only brightens up a picture, but also provides information. For example, with the color picture, students can see the actual color of things. Explain that artists use color to attract the viewer's attention and provide information about their subjects.

3. Give students a copy of the **Splashes of Color reproducible (page 86)**. Then set out magazines for the class. Show students examples of the many variations of one color. Then tell them to look through the magazines for a color they like and cut out various samples of that color. Have them glue all the pieces onto the paint can, mosaic style, until the can is covered with splashes of color.

4. Display the paint cans on a bulletin board for an eye-catching reminder that color plays an important part in our world.

Name _____ Date _____

Splashes of Color
Directions: Look through a magazine and cut out samples in a color you like. Try finding many different shades of that color. Glue your samples onto the paint can.

86 *Engage the Brain: Graphic Organizers and Other Visual Strategies • Grade 2*   *Reproducible*   978-1-4129-5226-2 • © Corwin Press

Splashes of Color

Directions: Look through a magazine and cut out samples in a color you like. Try finding many different shades of that color. Glue your samples onto the paint can.

Shades and Tints: Value Chart

Skills Objectives
Understand how shades and tints are produced.
Create shades and tints by mixing paint.

Materials
Shades and Tints reproducible

fabric swatches or paint chips of different shades and tints

tempera paint

paper plates

white paper

paintbrushes

newspaper

A **Value Chart** shows variations of one color by adding either black or white to make shades or tints. Creating a value chart provides students with hands-on experimentation and valuable practice in mixing colors. In this activity, students mix paint with black and white to see how shades and tints are produced.

1. Show students fabric swatches or paint chips that show different shades of a color. Point out that the samples are one color, but some are darker or lighter. Explain that the darker colors are called *shades* of the color, while the lighter colors are called *tints*.

2. Demonstrate how shades and tints are produced. Dab some blue tempera paint on a paper plate, and then paint a section of white paper. Show the paper to the class, and explain that this is the original color blue.

3. Next, add some black paint to the blue paint on the plate. Paint the new color on another sheet of paper. Point out the change in color. Then add more black paint to the blue on the plate, and paint the new color next to the last. Tell students that the darker colors are shades of blue.

4. Repeat Steps 2–3 with a new paper plate, but add white to the blue instead of black. Inform students that the lighter colors are tints of blue.

5. Tell students that they will be experimenting with shades and tints. Give them a copy of the **Shades and Tints reproducible (page 88)**. Cover work areas with newspaper, and set out the materials.

6. Instruct students to follow your procedure to make shades and tints. They will make shades of one color in the top row and tints of the same color in the bottom row.

7. When the paint is dry, arrange the papers on a bulletin board. Group them by color (all the blues together, all the greens, and so on). Your class will be amazed at the many different colors they produced!

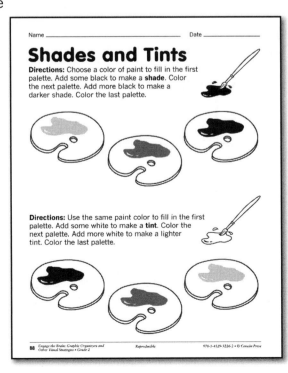

Name _____ Date _____

Shades and Tints

Directions: Choose a color of paint to fill in the first palette. Add some black to make a **shade**. Color the next palette. Add more black to make a darker shade. Color the last palette.

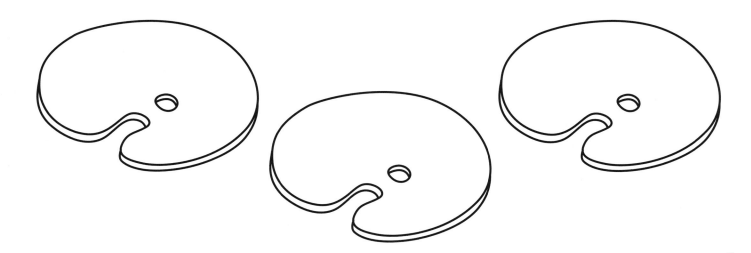

Directions: Use the same paint color to fill in the first palette. Add some white to make a **tint**. Color the next palette. Add more white to make a lighter tint. Color the last palette.

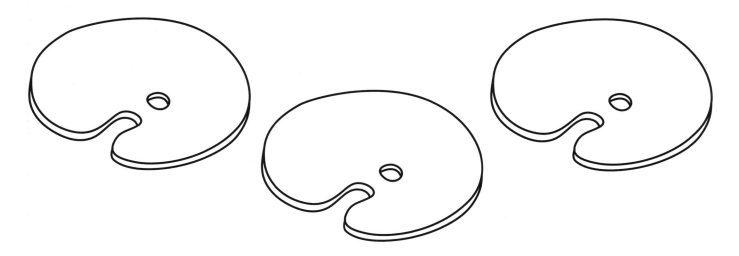

Reproducible 978-1-4129-5226-2 • © Corwin Press

Different Kinds of Lines: Sectioned Chart

Skills Objectives
Identify different kinds of lines.
Understand that artists use lines for different effects.

Materials
Lines Can
Be Different
reproducible

markers or pencils

chart paper

scissors

tape

Lines are one of the basic elements of art. Lines can take on many forms. They can be used to communicate pictures and express movement and emotion. A **Sectioned Chart** can help organize information or images. Students can use a sectioned chart to explore and note the differences among a variety of lines.

1. Ask a volunteer to draw a circle on the board. Then ask three other volunteers to draw a tree, a house, and a snake. Ask what the pictures have in common. Guide the class to see that all the pictures were created with lines.

2. Have students describe the lines that were used to make the pictures (e.g., *straight, curved, long, short, wiggly*). List the words on the board. Then draw other kinds of lines on the board (e.g., thick, thin, jagged, loopy, wavy), and have students suggest words to describe them. Add the new words to the list. Explain that there are many different kinds of lines.

3. Give students a copy of the **Lines Can Be Different reproducible (page 90)**. Read the directions together, and then instruct students to use markers or pencils to create interesting line designs in each box of their chart. Encourage them to extend their line designs across the length of the page.

4. Later, have students cut apart the four sections of their chart. Label sheets of chart paper *Jagged Lines*, *Curly Lines*, and so on. Ask students to tape their lines under the correct headings. Point out the variety of designs they created.

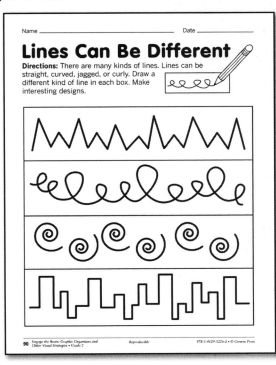

Lines Can Be Different

Directions: There are many kinds of lines. Lines can be straight, curved, jagged, or curly. Draw a different kind of line in each box. Make interesting designs.

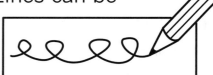

Music at Work: Poster

Skills Objectives

Identify the different places and situations where music is played.
Recognize that music has many purposes.
Identify effective communication through making a poster.

Materials
chart paper
worksheets
poster board
old magazines
art supplies

A **Poster** is an effective visual for advertising or communicating important information, such as the influence of music in our lives. Music is an important part of our culture, as well as a form of entertainment and art. It plays a vital role in special events, such as graduations, weddings, and religious services. In this activity, students explore how music is used in many places and situations.

1. In advance, tape a few worksheets with lots of small writing onto a piece of chart paper. Hold it up to the class, and ask if this poster is an effective tool to communicate information. Help them see that the text is too small to read from a distance, and there are not enough visual images or color.

2. Ask students to think about when they've heard music in the past week. List responses on the board (e.g., *on television or radio, in a store, at the doctor's office*). Tell students that music is an important part of our world, and they will make a poster to express the importance of music in their lives.

3. Divide the class into small groups. Have groups brainstorm and list all the different occasions in which music is played.

4. Have each group make a poster identifying the many ways music enriches our lives. A poster needs to be seen from far away, so images and text should be large and have strong color elements. Encourage students to use a variety of resources, including images from magazines or their own drawings or paintings. Encourage students to title their posters using large writing or cutout print. Before they begin, check to make sure students understand the assignment.

5. Suggest that students sketch out their ideas on scrap paper first, and then lay them out on the poster board before gluing on, drawing, or painting pictures.

6. Invite groups to share their posters with the class. Have them explain why they chose certain images and what message they were trying to convey.

All Kinds of Instruments: Circle Chart

Skills Objectives

Identify different kinds of musical instruments.

Recognize that instruments are played in different ways.

Understand that instruments may be grouped by how they are played.

Materials

Musical Instruments reproducible

musical recording featuring instruments

CD or cassette player

pictures and books featuring musical instruments

2 instruments from different categories (e.g., guitar and recorder)

butcher paper

Musical tones are produced when air vibrates. Where and how the vibrations are made affects the sound. In this activity, students explore how musical instruments produce different sounds. They use a **Circle Chart** to group instruments according to how they are played.

1. Play a musical recording, and have students identify the instruments they hear. List their responses on the board. Then read aloud the names of the instruments from the recording so students can check their guesses.

2. Discuss that there are many kinds of instruments. Then show an instrument such as a guitar. Ask students how the instrument is played, and play some notes on it. Show another instrument such as a recorder. Ask how that instrument is played, and play it as well. Explain that how an instrument is played influences the sounds it produces.

3. Give students a copy of the **Musical Instruments reproducible (page 93)**. Point out the four headings on the chart. Then divide the class into small groups, and have each group list several instruments for each heading. Let students refer to books or pictures of instruments to help them fill in the chart.

4. When students are finished, draw a large circle on butcher paper. Compile the information into one large chart. Have volunteers decorate the chart with drawings and pictures.

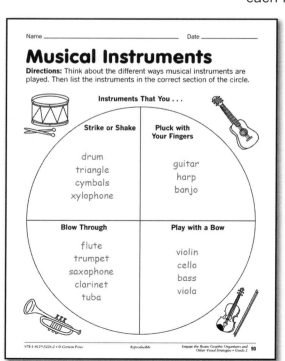

Name _____ Date _____

Musical Instruments

Directions: Think about the different ways musical instruments are played. Then list the instruments in the correct section of the circle.

Instruments That You . . .

Strike or Shake
drum
triangle
cymbals
xylophone

Pluck with Your Fingers
guitar
harp
banjo

Blow Through
flute
trumpet
saxophone
clarinet
tuba

Play with a Bow
violin
cello
bass
viola

978-1-4129-5226-2 • © Corwin Press   Reproducible   Engage the Brain: Graphic Organizers and Other Visual Strategies • Grade 2   93

Name _____   Date _____

Musical Instruments

Directions: Think about the different ways musical instruments are played. Then list the instruments in the correct section of the circle.

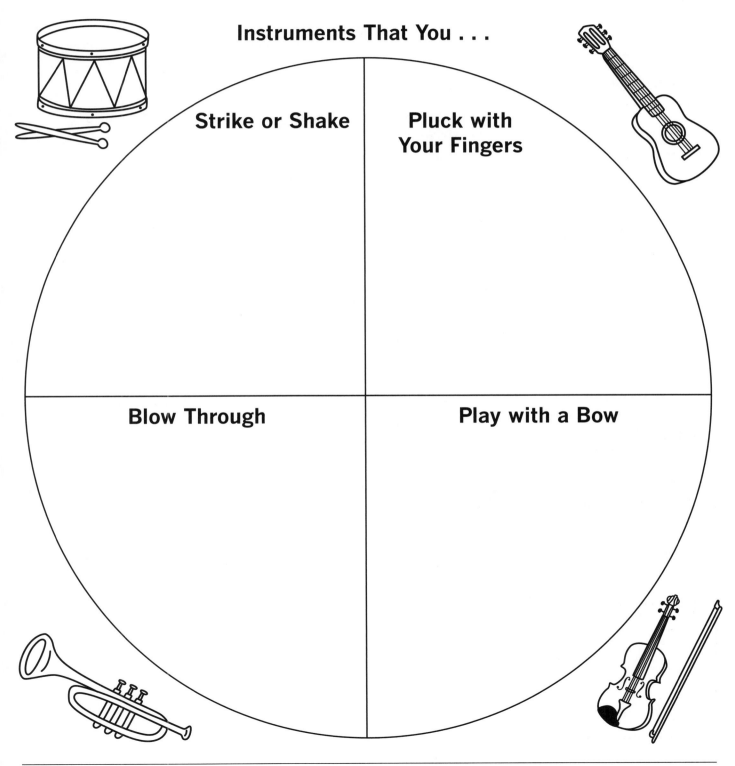

Instruments That You . . .

Strike or Shake

Pluck with Your Fingers

Blow Through

Play with a Bow

Songs for Different Reasons: Four-Column Chart

Materials

Songs I Know reproducible

various music selections on CD or audiotape

CD or cassette player

Skills Objectives

Recognize that songs are written or sung for different reasons.
Group together songs with similar purposes.

Songs make up a large part of students' exposure to music. Help students see that songs are not just something learned for a music program. In this activity, students recall songs they know and then categorize them into different groups using a **Four-Column Chart**. Each category reflects a particular purpose for the songs.

1. Play two different songs for the class. For example, play a lullaby (such as "Hush, Little Baby") and a silly song (such as "Hokey Pokey"). Talk about how the songs differ, for example: *One song is slow, and the other is fast. One song comforts you, and the other song makes you laugh.*

2. Guide the class to see that songs are written and sung for different purposes. Songs for fun, such as "Hokey Pokey," often contain made-up words and silly ideas that make people laugh. Other songs are more serious. National anthems, for example, are intended to stir up strong emotions in people. Some songs, such as commercial jingles, are meant to catch people's attention and sell products.

3. Give students a copy of the **Songs I Know reproducible (page 95)**. Discuss the four categories on the chart. (If you wish to change the categories, do so before reproducing the page.) Have the class suggest some songs that might fit into the categories.

4. Have partners work together to fill in the chart. Provide compact discs and audiotapes that students can refer to, and play some of the songs as students work.

5. When students are finished, invite them to share their charts with the class. Have "music time," and allow students to select some songs for the class to sing.

Songs I Know

Directions: Think of songs that fit in each group below. Write the titles of the songs in the chart.

Lullabies	Patriotic Songs	Silly Songs	Happy Songs

References

Aaron, H. J. (2002). Natural resources. In *World book encyclopedia* (Vol. 154, p. 64). Chicago, IL: World Book.

Allard, H. (1977). *Miss Nelson is missing!* Boston, MA: Houghton Mifflin.

Branch, W. D. (2002). Peanut. In *World book encyclopedia* (Vol. 15, pp. 213–215). Chicago, IL: World Book.

Cash, T., Parker, S., & Taylor, B. (1990). *175 More science experiments to amuse and amaze your friends.* New York, NY: Random House.

Claytor, C., & Potter, J. (1997). Matthew Henson. *African Americans who were first.* New York, NY: Dutton.

Col, J. (n.d.). *Graphic organizers.* Retrieved Sept. 18, 2006, from the Enchanted Learning Web site: http://www.enchantedlearning.com/graphicorganizers.

Croy, L. I. (2002). Wheat. In *World book encyclopedia* (Vol. 121, pp. 266–277). Chicago, IL: World Book.

Darling, K. (1997). *Rain forest babies.* New York, NY: Walker and Company.

Farndon, J. (1992). *How the earth works.* London, England: Dorling Kindersley.

Gallery, D., & Gallery, M. (n.d.). *Graphic organizers.* Retrieved September 18, 2006, from the Enchanted Learning Web site: http://www.enchantedlearning.com/graphicorganizers.

Gardner, H. (1983). *Frames of mind: The theory of multiple intelligences.* New York, NY: Basic Books.

Gorenstein, P. (2002). Moon. In *World book encyclopedia* (Vol. 13, pp. 790–791). Chicago, IL: World Book.

Hunt, W. R. (2002). Henson, Matthew Alexander. In *World book encyclopedia* (Vol. 9, p. 191). Chicago, IL: World Book.

Jensen, E., & Johnson, G. (1994). *The learning brain.* San Diego, CA: Turning Point for Teachers.

Kitchens, J. W. (2002). George Washington Carver. In *World book encyclopedia* (Vol. 3, pp. 268–269). Chicago, IL: World Book.

Ling, M. (1993). *Penguin.* London, England: Dorling Kindersley.

Longyear, R. M. (2002). Music. In *World book encyclopedia* (Vol. 13, pp. 948–949). Chicago, IL: World Book.

March, R. H. (2002). Matter. In *World book encyclopedia* (Vol. 13, p. 311). Chicago, IL: World Book.

McCarthy, B. National Council for the Social Studies. (2002). *Expectations of excellence: Curriculum standards for social studies.* Silver Spring, MD: National Council for the Social Studies.

National Council of Teachers of English and International Reading Association. (1996). *Standards for the English language arts.* Urbana, IL: National Council of Teachers of English.

National Council of Teachers of Mathematics. (2005). *Principles and standards for school mathematics.* Reston, VA: National Council of Teachers of Mathematics.

National Grain and Feed Association™. (n.d.). *Wheat: From farm to table.* Retrieved October 15, 2006, from http://www.ngfa.org/wheat.htm.

National Research Council. (2005). *National science education standards.* Washington, DC: National Academy Press.

Ogle, D. M. (2000). Make it visual: A picture is worth a thousand words. In M. McLaughlin & M. Vogt (Eds.), *Creativity and innovation in content area teaching.* Norwood, MA: Christopher-Gordon.

Tate, M. L. (2003). *Worksheets don't grow dendrites: 20 instructional strategies that engage the brain.* Thousand Oaks, CA: Corwin Press.

Van de Walle, J. A. (2004). Developing place-value concepts and procedures. *Elementary and middle school mathematics: Teaching developmentally.* Boston, MA: Pearson Education.

Wyszecki, G. (2002). Color. In *World book encyclopedia* (Vol. 4, p. 822). Chicago, IL: World Book.